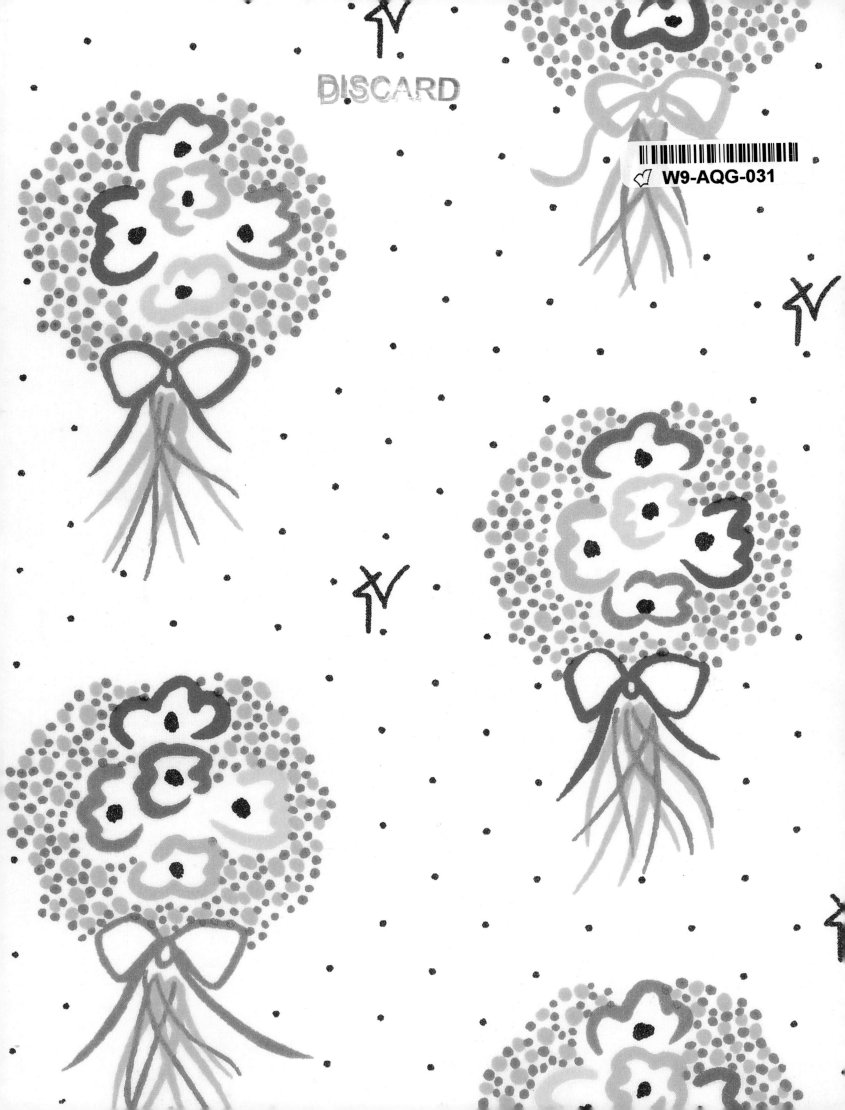

THE WORLD OF
GLORIA VANDERBILT

R. C. VANDERBILTS HAVE A DAUGHTER

Grandchild of Mrs. Vanderbilt Fourth in Line From Founder of Family.

WAS BORN IN A HOSPITAL

Mother Is the Former Gloria Morgan, Who Was Married Here in Last March.

Mr. and Mrs. Reginald Claypool Vanderbilt are being congratulated on the birth of a daughter yesterday at the Lying-In Hospital, Stuyvesant Square. Mrs. Vanderbilt was Miss Gloria Mercedes Morgan, one of the twin daughters

THE WORLD OF

Gloria Vanderbilt

BY WENDY GOODMAN

WITH A FOREWORD BY ANDERSON COOPER

ABRAMS, NEW YORK

NEW PHOTOGRAPHY BY DITTE ISAGER

ART DIRECTION AND DESIGN BY CHIP KIDD

PHOTOGRAPHY EDITING BY PHILIP REESER

gloria vanderbilt

CONTENTS

FOREWORD

My mom comes from a time and a place that no longer exist. The world she was born into, the world she managed to escape from, seems so distant to us now. I used to think of her as an emissary from some distant solar system; a visitor to our shores. In this world, but not necessarily of it.

"A fatherless girl thinks all things possible and nothing safe." Mary Gordon wrote that, and over the years my mom quoted it often. As a child, I didn't quite understand what it meant, how it applied to her. Now of course, I do. I think it explains a lot.

When you have lost, as a child, a father, a mother; when you are raised with the terrible knowledge that nothing is what it seems, and nothing can protect you, you come to understand that anything is possible, anything can happen. Great pain, great pleasure. There is no safety in guarantees.

My mother learned that lesson early on. She was born in 1924 into a world of unwritten rules, great wealth, and personal deprivation. Her father died when she was still an infant. Her mother—young and beautiful—was completely unprepared to be a parent. At ten, my mother was the subject of a custody dispute. Her aunt, Gertrude Vanderbilt Whitney, succeeded in taking her away from her own mother, and my mom lost her beloved nurse as well. The trial was a tabloid sensation. It was my mother's first taste of fame, and the hurt that often comes with it. She somehow survived and, unmoored, began a journey that has taken her through many lives, many loves, many losses.

Years ago I asked her how she had survived. "I had an image of myself that at my core there was a rock-hard diamond that nothing could get at, nothing could crack," she said. It was not a boast, it was a statement of fact, a sentence suffused with sadness.

My mom is a survivor, but she has none of the toughness that term often implies. She has strength, great stores of it, but she has refused to develop a layer of thick skin to protect herself. She remains vulnerable. It is a difficult and some-times painful choice. She wants to remain open—open eyes, open mind, open heart. It's cost her, but she has succeeded. There is no one I know who is so open to the new: new experiences, new opportunities, new love, even if it means new loss. She truly believes the best is yet to come, that great adventures are out there, just around the corner. She may have been born into a world that no longer exists, but she lives in a place about to happen.

At eighty-six, she is the most youthful person I know; also the most modern. She is cool, but doesn't take herself too seriously. When I suggested she remove a particularly racy passage from one of her memoirs, she giggled at my caution, and my dour tone. The paragraph went to print.

Someone recently asked her if she was happy. "The rainbow comes and goes," she replied. It does for all of us, I suppose, but what is remarkable about the woman you will discover in these pages is that she still believes the rainbow is out there. If she can't see it, she creates it for herself.

I wrote that I used to see her as an emissary from a distant star. Now, I see her as a dancer on a high-wire. She moves along softly, balanced above the crowd, in and out of the spotlight. She is dazzling, surprising, free from constraints. She looks back, she smiles broadly, she skips forward. Her eyes are focused straight ahead.

—**Anderson Cooper**

OPPOSITE:
A page from one of Gloria's many family albums shows her with Anderson when he was a baby. Later, when he was first learning to write, Anderson added the hearts and the words "Love" and "Mummy."

LOVE

MUMMY

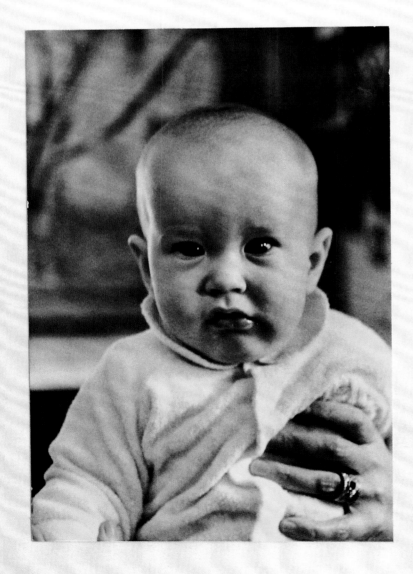

INTRODUCTION

The first time I remember seeing Gloria Vanderbilt was at a Christmas party. I must have been about nine years old. She had just taken off her coat and was arranging her hair in the mirror of Stuart Scheftel and Geraldine Fitzgerald's entrance hall. She was wearing a gray cashmere dress with bright red stockings and flat shoes, no jewelry. I was mesmerized. It wasn't just that she was so beautiful and I had never seen a grown-up in red stockings before; she seemed linked to a world of untamed glamour that made her totally mysterious.

To this day that image of Gloria Vanderbilt has stayed with me. Two years ago during lunch at Gloria's apartment I noticed a photograph of her draped over the arm of a sofa in a grand room—a dark angel lost in thought. The photograph was taken by her friend Richard Avedon in the 1950s, when Gloria was married to Sidney Lumet and they lived at 10 Gracie Square. I asked if there were more photographs like that and Gloria said that yes, there were. Gloria has kept her own extensive archive, and she has been photographed by almost every legendary fashion photographer of the twentieth century, but it was that one Avedon photograph that said everything to me, igniting the idea for this book. I felt that there needed to be a visual biography of Gloria's extraordinary life. She has been in the public eye since the day she was born. There has always been a fascination with her legendary beauty and originality, but the story beyond that is how Gloria Vanderbilt has emerged from her complicated family history to triumph as a thoroughly modern working mother and artist, driven by her determination and discipline. Gloria Vanderbilt is always moving forward at the speed of light with renewed purpose, harnessing her myriad talents to the challenges and new currents around her every single day.

—Wendy Goodman

15.

OPPOSITE:
Richard Avedon and Gloria Vanderbilt first met in the early 1950s, and would remain friends until his death in 2004. Avedon took this portrait of Gloria in 1956, when she lived in the South Penthouse at 10 Gracie Square with her husband Sidney Lumet and her two boys, Stan and Christopher Stokowski. Her portrait by John Carroll hangs above the sofa, and one of her own paintings hangs above the side table.

1.

GROWING UP VANDERBILT

"I'm glad I don't have that last name; it just comes with baggage and not much else."

—ANDERSON COOPER,
INTERVIEW WITH THE AUTHOR ON SEPTEMBER 25, 2009

OPPOSITE:
Among the few mementos of Gloria's father, Reginald Claypoole Vanderbilt, are a photograph of her with him when she was about a year old and a box of his woven name tags, probably from when he was in college. The gold cigarette case is inscribed with several monograms added over the years as it was passed down to family members. Gloria's father had originally given it to his mother-in-law, Laura Kilpatrick Morgan, who in turn gave it to her granddaughter, Gloria, who then gave it to Pat De Cicco when they married in 1941. It was returned to her only after De Cicco's death; when she opened it, Gloria found that he had kept a photograph of her inside all those years.

This is where my beloved nurse, Dodo, brought me from the hospital," Gloria Vanderbilt says softly, standing in the entrance hall of 12 East Seventy-seventh Street, the townhouse that belonged to her father at the time of her birth. It has been eighty-six years since that day, and she has not been back until this visit. The house is now owned by Brandeis University, serving as the alumni headquarters in New York City. Gloria has returned to see the house at the invitation of the president of the Alumni Association, Allen Alter, and to view a photo album discovered there that belonged to her father. The album shows each room of the townhouse as it was decorated when he lived there in the early 1920s, including the room where her father proposed to her mother.

Her father, Reginald Claypoole Vanderbilt, was forty-two years old when he invited her mother, Mercedes Morgan, to come to dinner at this house in 1922. She was seventeen at the time (or so she had been led to believe by her mother, who maintained that she was born in 1905; the actual date was 1904). Reggie, as he was familiarly known, had also invited his good friend Maury Paul to join them. As "Cholly Knickerbocker," the society columnist for the *New York Journal-American*, Paul was a powerful ally, even for a Vanderbilt. *Life* magazine dubbed Knickerbocker a "living encyclopedia of society history."[1] He coined the phrase "café society" to describe the infiltration of new money redefining the social landscape previously ordained by Gilded Age matriarchs like Mrs. William Astor. Mercedes and her identical twin sister, Thelma, had already appeared in his column as the "Magical Morgans"; he called Mercedes simply "Glorious Gloria." (Mercedes changed her name to Gloria in grade school, as she didn't like the nickname "Mercy," given to her by her classmates.)[2]

That night, Knickerbocker sensed he was about to get one of the biggest scoops of his career, but neither he nor Gloria could have known what she was about to hear. Reggie outlined the situation. "I love you; I want to marry you—but I want you to know exactly where you stand. All I have is a trust fund from my father of $5 million. When I die, that goes to Cathleen, or to other children if I have them. My physician tells me I am a sick man, and in all probability there will be no issue from this marriage. The chances are you would be a Mrs. Vanderbilt with no money. Do you understand exactly what I am saying to you?"[3] If this came as a shock, Gloria never let on. She persuaded him that she was not in the least bit daunted by the news. She was in love with Reggie and made it clear that the only thing that would deter her from the marriage was the disapproval of his mother, Mrs. Cornelius Vanderbilt II.

Gloria and Thelma had been so used to fending for themselves that even with this warning, marriage into one of the country's most powerful dynasties to a man she genuinely loved must have felt like a fairy tale come true. The ravishing sisters were not yet eighteen when they made the bold decision, in 1921, to flee their nomadic family life in Europe and set down roots by themselves in New York City. They had found an apartment in a brownstone at 40 Fifth Avenue and lived on an allowance of $200 a month provided by their father. They dove into the social season, attending nightclubs like the Montmartre; coming-out parties, notably including one for Cathleen Vanderbilt, Reggie's daughter by his first marriage to Cathleen Neilson; and tea dances at the Plaza Hotel.

Their bachelorette days, however, were short-lived. By the time Gloria met Reggie in the winter of 1922, Thelma had already eloped with James Vail Converse Jr., a grandson of James Converse, of the Bell Telephone family. Their mother, Laura Valdivieso Kilpatrick Morgan, might have expressed more enthusiasm for

18.

OPPOSITE:
Gloria and Thelma Morgan: the celebrated twin sisters dubbed the "Magical Morgans" by society columnist Cholly Knickerbocker. They were the toast of New York and Europe in the early 1920s. They coauthored their autobiography, *Double Exposure*, in 1958. Gloria's mother also wrote an autobiography, *Without Prejudice*, with Palma Wayne in 1936.

20.

OPPOSITE:

The library in Reginald Vanderbilt's New York City townhouse at 12 East Seventy-seventh Street at the time he met Gloria's mother in 1922. He proposed marriage to her in the downstairs clubroom of this house. The house now belongs to Brandeis University.

PHOTO BY HAAS

HILL'S STUDIO
N. Y. C.

the news had she not been distracted by the failure of her ambitious matchmaking for the twins' elder sister, Consuelo, whose marriage to Count Jean de Maupas had been an unhappy one from the start.

The serene, untouchable beauties portrayed in early photographs of Gloria and Thelma give no hint of the tumultuous days of their youth, spent in the company of their erratic and overbearing mother. The twins' decision to come to New York was as much about liberation from her as it was about the adventures they dreamed of in the glamorous city. Laura Morgan was fixated on one thing: money. Her determination to marry off her daughters to men of means clearly was as much for her own insurance as it was for theirs. She was a force of nature and would not be deterred from anything she set her mind to do. Today Gloria remembers her grandmother as "diminutive, intense, ever expressing the raging fires of the crazed obsessions within her passionate heart. Dodo [Gloria's affectionate nickname for her childhood nurse] called her 'the Little Countess' and said she was 'capable of blowing up the subways.' Quite true, not an exaggeration. The beautiful long hair I see in her photographs had been cut short and touched up into a coppery orange. She had, and it remained so to the end of her life, the most translucent, exquisite skin I have ever seen. Like my mother and Aunt Thelma, her nails were expertly manicured and lacquered mahogany-red."[4]

Until Thelma's marriage to Converse, the twins were inseparable—but Gloria did not find herself alone for long. She was introduced to the famous heir and divorcé Reginald Vanderbilt at a dinner party given by her sister on a snowy winter night shortly after Thelma's wedding. After a brief courtship, Reggie gave fair warning with his proposal, and the date was set. Gloria was so determined to go through with the marriage that she concealed how ill she felt on the day of her wedding, March 6, 1923.

That night, when she and Reggie arrived at Sandy Point Farm, his estate in Portsmouth, Rhode Island, after what should have been a romantic journey in the Vanderbilt private railroad car, she collapsed with a severe case of diphtheria. The tables had turned on the newlyweds; it was Gloria, not Reggie, who was in real peril. It took her three months to recover. By then, Reggie was already trapped in a catastrophe of his own making, suffering from cirrhosis of the liver and ignoring his doctor's warning that if he did not stop drinking, he was courting death. But fate intervened, and they were able to conceive a child.

"I was ecstatically happy," Gloria wrote of her pregnancy in her autobiography. "I wanted to give him a son to be called Reginald Vanderbilt, Jr."[5] Instead, she gave him a daughter. Gloria Laura Morgan Vanderbilt was born in New York City on February 20, 1924, bearing the names of both her mother and grandmother. Baby Gloria's grandmother was even in the operating room during the birth, by cesarean section. "Even here the air was thick with contention. Like witnesses to a royal birth where substitution of an heir to a throne is feared, Mamma insisted on

OPPOSITE:

Baby Gloria, in her christening gown, with her mother in 1924. Looking at the pearls encircling her mother's neck, today Gloria remembers, "My paternal grandmother had a long string of pearls; one day they were at Delmonico's for lunch, and she said, 'All Vanderbilt women have to have pearls.' She asked the waiter for some scissors, cut them off, and just handed them to my mother."

being present at the operation."[6] (In those days birth by cesarean section was risky, and Laura Morgan would have been understandably frightened for her daughter.)

Baby Gloria's parents immediately departed for Europe, not to return until August. She was left in the care of her maternal grandmother, whom she always referred to as Naney (pronounced "Nanny"), who had joined her daughters in America, and an Irish nurse, Emma Keislich, always called "Dodo." The latter was never once to leave her charge's side from the minute she was hired, when Gloria was two weeks old, until she was dismissed during Gloria's custody trial in 1934. These two women would become the closest thing to a real, nurturing family in the early years of Gloria's nomadic childhood, already so similar to the rootless upbringing her own mother had endured.

Gloria Vanderbilt's birth must have seemed like a small miracle to her mother and ailing father. Reggie was larger than life. Gloria's mother wrote, "As for Reggie, he was not born a Vanderbilt for nothing; it had given him all that the name implies—but not all the wealth in the world could ever give him that gentle,

ABOVE LEFT:
A detail of Reginald Claypoole Vanderbilt's dinner service

ABOVE RIGHT:
A view of the main house at Sandy Point Farm, Gloria's father's estate in Portsmouth, Rhode Island, which was much more relaxed than The Breakers, his parents' mansion in Newport. Here he had a stable and an indoor riding ring for his horses, as well as kennels for his dogs. Reginald founded the United States Equestrian Federation. "The house was torn down some years ago," says Gloria. "Now only the stables remain."

darling heart of his. He was the kindest, tenderest human being I have ever met."[7]
He acted as a buffer between his bride and her tyrannical mother, who was invited
along with Thelma to join the family at Sandy Point Farm.

At nineteen, Mrs. Reginald Vanderbilt was folded into a world of unimag-
inable luxury and social protocol, although Sandy Point Farm was much more
relaxed and informal than The Breakers and other Vanderbilt outposts in Newport.
Reggie had neither the time nor patience for the stilted conventions of the society
into which he was born. Early on, he fashioned his own free-spirited routine
according to his tastes, which included a love of horses, cars, and gambling. Sandy
Point Farm's 280 acres comprised the main house, many cottages, and a magnificent stable with an indoor riding ring, where he kept sixty horses, as well as
kennels that stretched out over an acre for his dogs.[8] The Vanderbilts had maintained their hold on society and industry through four powerful generations. They
stood at the summit of American royalty in the twilight of the Gilded Age. Gloria
Vanderbilt was born an heiress, the great-great-granddaughter of Cornelius

OPPOSITE:
Anderson Cooper now owns his
grandfather's silver champion horse
show trophies.

ABOVE:
An aerial view of Sandy Point Farm

LEFT:
The interior of Reginald Vanderbilt's
stables at Sandy Point Farm with
monogrammed feed buckets

Vanderbilt, known as "the Commodore." From his humble, rural beginnings on Staten Island in 1794, this founder of the Vanderbilt dynasty had built the greatest family fortune in America.

With his brilliant business instinct and fearless character, the Commodore became the model of the capitalist adventurer. He went from running a simple ferry business to owning steamships, and by the time he formed the American Atlantic and Pacific Ship Canal Company in 1849, he was already a millionaire.[9] Although he was considered crude and was shunned by the established society of his day, he did not lack the vanity of wanting to indulge in the rewards of his ever-increasing wealth. In 1852 he built a private 270-foot yacht, *The North Star*, with splendid Louis XV salons and ten luxurious staterooms.[10] He was domineering and ruled his family with an iron will. In 1846, when his wife, Sophia, resisted moving from Staten Island into the new mansion he had built for her and their thirteen children on Washington Place in Manhattan, he had her committed to the Bloomingdale Insane Asylum until she changed her mind.[11] In 1863, he took control of the New York and Harlem Railroad (now known as the Metro-North Railroad).

After Sophia died in 1868, Vanderbilt married Frank Armstrong Crawford, a Southern belle forty-five years his junior.[12] In 1873 he commenced construction on Grand Central Terminal in New York City. His statue stands today outside the south side of the building. When he died in 1877, he was worth $100 million. He left the largest portion of this vast fortune to his son William Henry, Gloria's great-grandfather. William's son, Cornelius II, Gloria's grandfather and Reggie's father, received $5 million.[13]

As the fortunes of the Vanderbilt men rose, so did the ambitions of their wives. The legendary rivalry between Reggie's mother, Alice Claypoole Gwynne, and Alva Erskine Smith, the wife of his uncle, William Kissam Vanderbilt, initiated a building spree that produced some of the most spectacular residential architecture in America. By 1879 plans had been drawn up by William Henry to build a double mansion on the west side of Fifth Avenue between Fifty-first

29.

OPPOSITE:
Gloria's great-great-grandfather, Cornelius "Commodore" Vanderbilt, founded the family dynasty with his gifts as a maverick capitalist. He was born on a farm in Staten Island in 1794 and started his financial ascent as a youth running a ferry business between Staten Island and Manhattan. When he died in 1877, he had founded the New York Central and Hudson River Railway line, initiating the building of the first Grand Central Terminal. He had amassed a fortune of $100 million.

and Fifty-second Streets, at 640 Fifth Avenue. William Henry, his wife, Maria
Louisa, and their youngest son were to live in one house while their two daughters and their families were to live in the adjoining mansion. The Herter Brothers
were hired to decorate the interiors. Their cabinetry workshops were famous
for designing grand-scale Gothic- and Renaissance-revival furnishings for the
castles of the newly crowned kings of industry. Soon Fifth Avenue's prime real
estate would become the Vanderbilts' very own urban kingdom, with castles to
rival any European royalty. William Kissam and Alva enlisted Richard Morris
Hunt to build a chateau in the French Renaissance style at 660 Fifth Avenue, on
the corner of Fifty-second Street, just north of 640 Fifth. It was completed in 1882.
Alva hosted a spectacular housewarming in 1883, with a fancy-dress ball for 1,200
guests[14] that displayed such unprecedented wealth and lavish entertaining that
she disarmed her rivals, notably Mrs. Astor, whom she unseated that night as the
reigning queen of New York society. Alva was dressed as a Venetian princess for
the ball, while her brother-in-law, Cornelius Vanderbilt II, went as Louis XVI.
His wife, Alice, caused a sensation with a dress that lit up as she portrayed "the
spirit of Electricity," to celebrate the new invention of electric light.

Not to be outdone, Cornelius and Alice hired George Browne Post to design
their chateau on the corner of Fifty-seventh Street and Fifth Avenue. The first

ABOVE & OPPOSITE:
Vanderbilt palaces lined Fifth Avenue,
culminating in Cornelius II and Alice's
mansion between Fifty-seventh and Fifty-
eighth Streets—now the site of Bergdorf
Goodman and Van Cleef & Arpels. The
original house was built by architect
George Browne Post at 1 West Fifty-
seventh Street in 1882. Ten years later, the
Vanderbilts asked Post, along with Richard
Morris Hunt, to extend and redesign the
house after they bought and demolished
the five remaining brownstones on the
avenue. The result was their new 130-
room palace, complete with a grand porte
cochere and forty servants. Alice Vanderbilt
sold the house in 1925 for $7 million.

house was completed in 1883. Three years later they enlarged the property to cover the entire block from Fifty-seventh to Fifty-eighth Streets on Fifth Avenue (the site of Van Cleef & Arpels and Bergdorf Goodman today) with a $3-million addition by Post along with his mentor, Richard Morris Hunt, consulting on the design. Eight hundred workers completed the mansion of 130 rooms in two years.[15] The *New York Times* called it "the Finest Private Residence in America."[16] This was the house where Reggie grew up, and where Gloria Morgan would first meet her future mother-in-law.

The rivalry between Alice and Alva didn't stop at Fifth Avenue. In Newport, Alva commissioned Hunt to build a copy of the Petit Trianon at Versailles. Her summer "cottage" was called Marble House, the gold ballroom by Jules Allard et Fils designed to evoke the hall of mirrors at Versailles.[17] Alice, too, hired Hunt to build an Italian Renaissance palace that dominated the shoreline on a magnificent site. The Breakers remains one of the most glorious examples of Gilded Age architecture in America. The new American royals were families who made up their own social rules. They invented coats of arms, and however authentic those might have looked, power and money, not family trees, now determined who ruled.

Laura Morgan, on the other hand, didn't have this golden parachute of privilege in her family background. But what she lacked in fortune she made up in temperament. Her father was Hugh Judson Kilpatrick, a Union officer who fought under General Sherman in the Civil War and earned the rank of major general. He met Laura's mother, Luisa Valdivieso, in 1867 during his term as United States Minister in Chile. With his feisty character, he would have been a good match for the Commodore.

Laura was married in 1897, at the age of thirty-one, to the diplomat Harry Hays Morgan. "My grandfather, Harry Hays Morgan, was born in New Orleans," Gloria says. "The family owned a large plantation—the Aurora—an especially famous one on the Mississippi, which yielded an income for many years. Even when my grandfather inherited his share of it, it brought in a good yearly check—and it was that and not the government one that allowed my grandmother Morgan [Naney] the indulgences of the many ocean trips consular salaries are not flexible

Laura Kip Schick
New York
1897.

OPPOSITE:

A portrait of Luisa Valdivieso, mother of Laura Kilpatrick Morgan

ABOVE:

Gloria's maternal great-grandfather, Hugh Judson Kilpatrick, who was a major general in the Union Army during the American Civil War. He was appointed an ambassador to Chile in 1865 by President Andrew Jackson. There he met and married his second wife, Luisa Valdivieso.

enough to permit. His father, my great-grandfather Morgan, was a judge of the Supreme Court of Louisiana and was appointed Judge to the International Court of Alexandria, Egypt—and after that was given his portfolio as American Minister to Mexico."[18]

Their children were born in Lucerne, Switzerland, where Morgan was stationed in the early years of their marriage. First came Harry in 1898, followed by Consuelo in 1902, and then Thelma and Gloria in 1904. Laura Morgan's volatile temper and erratic behavior manifested in unpredictable ways. She abandoned Consuelo when the girl was just fourteen, leaving her at the home of Edith and George Gould in New Jersey, presumably to benefit from their solid, well-to-do household. From the age of twelve, Thelma and Gloria were shuttled to New York to board at the Convent of the Sacred Heart. Just two years after leaving boarding school at fifteen, the twins were allowed to live on their own in New York City without a chaperone. For such a controlling, manipulative mother, there is no accounting for such negligent behavior.

In her autobiographies *Without Prejudice* and *Double Exposure*, Gloria Morgan Vanderbilt outlined disturbing patterns of behavior by her mother that she unknowingly or unconsciously seems to have repeated with her own child. She wrote, "There can be no normal living in a scrambled existence—you strike at the very soundness of family life when you rob it of its even keel."[19] For young Gloria, her daughter, there was never an even keel. She relived the same insecurity and uprooting that her mother had experienced. As a child she felt that she had lost her mother to a life she observed but never shared. Today Gloria says, "I had no sense of the family I was born into. My mother, Naney Morgan, and my Aunt Gertrude never mentioned my father to me or talked about him. Only Dodo gave me some sense of him."[20] Her memoir *Once Upon a Time* opens with a chilling, heartbreaking sentence: "Once upon a time long ago I lay in my crib at Sandy Point Farm while my father lay in the next room dying."[21]

The end came on September 4, 1925, when Gloria's mother was in New York en route to South America, where her grandmother Kilpatrick was gravely ill. When she called to check in with her husband, who had not been feeling well earlier, a nurse answered the phone, announcing, "Mr. Vanderbilt has had a slight hemorrhage."[22] She raced back to Sandy Point, only to arrive two minutes after her husband died. The sweetness of the life he had given her was over.

OPPOSITE:
A rare photograph of Gloria with both of her parents, shortly before her father's death in 1925

PAGES 40–41:
Gloria and her nurse Dodo in front of The Breakers following her father's death in 1925

38.

2.

LEARNING THE SONGS OF THE CARAVAN

"I longed fervently for the day when I would be in the mysterious land of Grown-Up. There it would be different—I would have control."
—GLORIA VANDERBILT, INTERVIEW
WITH THE AUTHOR ON FEBRUARY 13, 2009

Gloria Vanderbilt sits in her book-lined dining room looking through family albums. She picks up a photograph of herself at age seven. "I thought, 'I know that person, and I am ready to write about her,' and that is how I started to write my book."[1] That book, *Once Upon a Time*, published in 1985, is the first of several autobiographical works. It reads like a fairy tale, but the heroine rides a dangerous current, as nothing in the story is make-believe. Gloria continues looking at this photograph of a young girl with rosy cheeks, wearing a hat dusted with snow. "This is something that [Judge] James A. Foley said [to my mother] before the battle

started." She reads: "'Do you know what a trial of this caliber can do? There will be so much dirt by the press that it will drag you and the child through a mire of infamy that will cling to her as long as she lives.'"[2] She pauses and says, "And that is true, and I have spent the rest of my life trying to make it okay."[3]

It is as if the room has been frosted with the snow in the photograph. Gloria continues: "Another quote from my mother's book. My grandmother Morgan said to my mother, 'If you will permit her to live with Mrs. Whitney, I feel sure Mrs. Whitney will give you fifty thousand dollars for life if you consent to this.'"[4] Gloria closes the book and says, "And I wish to God she had, which would have permitted Dodo, the only mother I knew, to remain by my side. And if it wasn't enough, she should have given her more until she accepted. As I have written in my book, it all started because I overheard my aunt [Consuelo] saying to my mother, 'You have to get rid of that nurse; what she needs is a German fräulein!' And Dodo was my life! She was the only mother I had. I felt panic and anger, terrible anger to all of them, except Dodo and Naney, without understanding why. It was as if a bomb had exploded, shattering my life apart. And later—much later—guilt. All orphans feel it is their fault."[5]

The custody trial in 1934, the defining moment in young Gloria Vanderbilt's life, was the ideal distraction for a society demoralized by the Great Depression and still reeling from the infamous kidnapping and murder of the baby of

OPPOSITE:
"Horror, horror, horror," Gloria says seventy-six years later, looking at this photograph of herself and a detective, taken during the custody trial between her mother and her aunt Gertrude Vanderbilt Whitney in 1934.

BELOW:
Letters written by Gloria to her grandmother during the custody trial. "My grandmother made me write this. She was masterminding what I wrote to use in the court case. I felt something was not quite right, but I wanted to please her."

45.

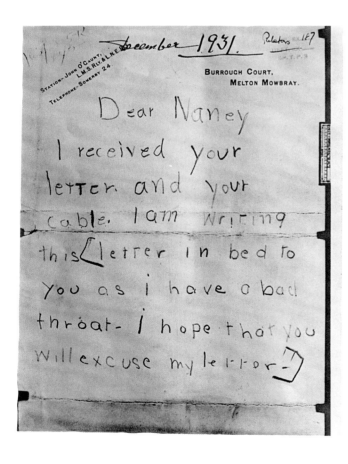

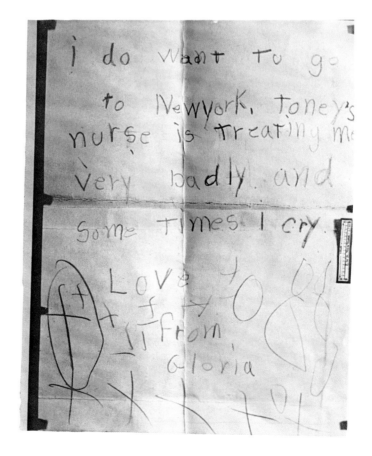

46.

America's hero, Charles Lindbergh. The trial stoked the fires of tabloid hell daily with lurid revelations and the ultimate Shakespearean betrayal, a mother turning against her own daughter. The papers were saturated with exposés about how the glamorous Vanderbilt widow lived, and how she and her royal European friends indulged in an allegedly degenerate lifestyle; Judge Foley's warning to Gloria's mother turned out to be frighteningly accurate. The trial was also the beginning of the public's obsession with the young heiress, who learned at the age of ten that there was nobody in the world she could depend on except that girl with the rosy cheeks wearing the hat dusted with snow.

Who could resist the enchanting, shy child in the eye of the perfect storm? Not the media, that was for sure. It was impossible for the public to think that with all that money, and all those houses filled with flowers, silver, and who knew what else, misery could follow a girl who was neglected, frightened, and desperate to figure out how to save her only lifeline—what she called "the Caravan," consisting of her grandmother Naney, and her beloved nurse Dodo.

The Caravan took shape immediately after Reggie's death, when baby Gloria, nineteen months old, was whisked away with Dodo to The Breakers, her grand-mother Vanderbilt's mansion in Newport, while funeral arrangements were made and her mother was deciding the next steps in her life. In her loving hugeness

ABOVE:
Baby Gloria with her nurse Dodo and her mother at Sandy Point Farm

OPPOSITE:
Gloria on horseback at about age ten. "I was trying to be close to my father by taking up riding. The only person who ever told me about him was Dodo. No one else. Not even my aunt [her father's own sister]. Aunt Gertrude was totally incapable of raising children. When I went to live with Aunt Gertrude at Old Westbury, none of her children welcomed me. I felt like a changeling, totally unrelated."

OPPOSITE:
A photograph of Gloria taken by Dodo

ABOVE:
Gloria made this painting when she was ten years old, while she was at the Greenvale School in Long Island.

Dodo was Gloria's "Big Elephant," her comfort and her protector. Gloria would eventually come to know that it was her own fortune, a portion of the $5-million inheritance Reggie had told Gloria Morgan their child would receive, which was the driving force behind her mother's lifestyle during her childhood. Young Gloria lived with one constant terror, that the Caravan was in peril of being disbanded—and that was unthinkable. The Caravan was the heartbeat of Gloria's life. Today she says, "The Caravan was home to three—Dodo, Naney, and me. It was steamer trunks, packing and unpacking on ocean liners, in hotels, on trains, in rented houses in Paris, Cannes, England—it mattered not where as long as we three were together."[6]

Gloria's childhood odyssey began in 1926 in Paris, where she lived in a house on avenue Charles Floquet[7] with her mother, Naney, Dodo, Aunt Thelma, and a staff that included Fernand (the butler) and her mother's personal maid, Marie. Gloria became enthralled by the rituals of her mother's preparation for evenings out, all under the watchful eye of Naney, who was keen to help her daughter navigate European society. After all, her daughter was a very young, very beautiful widow with her whole life ahead of her.

It was not surprising that baby Gloria's mother should have been drawn back to Paris after her husband's death. She had spent much of her youth in Europe, and the memories of her trips to Paris with Reggie were still fresh. With Reggie, she had stayed at the Ritz, dined at Maxim's, and met Lord Marmaduke Furness, one of the richest men in England, who would become Thelma's second husband. There had been luncheon parties at the house of the Maharaja of Kapurthala, where Mrs. Reginald Vanderbilt was dazzled by a wall tapestry made entirely of precious gems, as well as the durbar turban, containing the largest known emerald in the world, weighing 500 carats.[8]

Reggie's death left his young widow in the hands of a legal team assembled on the pretext that she was not yet of legal age, thanks to her mother's deception. Gloria's mother was, in fact, twenty-one years old at the time of Reggie's death, and therefore entitled to guardianship of Gloria's inheritance. But as she believed

50.

OPPOSITE:
Gloria driving a pedal car in Paris, with the Eiffel Tower in the background. Her mother had moved the family to Paris in 1926 after Reginald's death. Gloria led a nomadic life in Europe until she returned to America in 1932.

that she was still a minor, she enlisted George Wickersham of the firm Cadwalader, Wickersham & Taft to be her attorney. Thomas Gilchrist, an attorney in the same firm, read Reggie's will and advised her not to take the $500,000 left to her therein, as the money would have been instantly consumed by her husband's debts.[9] What she did have rights to were the proceeds from the sale of his properties, Sandy Point Farm and the townhouse at 12 East Seventy-seventh Street.

The eventual sale of these homes brought in $130,000. The $5-million trust left to Gloria and her now-married half-sister, Cathleen Cushing, was divided, and Gloria's share was controlled by Judge James Foley, a surrogate of the New York court,[10] who ruled that the child's mother was to receive $4,000 a month for Gloria's care. He also granted the widow's request to take her daughter and live in Europe.

Forty-eight thousand dollars a year was bounty enough to enjoy a charmed life in Europe in 1926, the value of the dollar being roughly twelve times what it is today. Thelma was about to marry Lord Furness and establish residence in his London mansion and at Burrough Court, his country estate near Melton Mowbray, very close to where Edward, Prince of Wales, loved to spend time at Fort Belvedere, on the edge of Windsor Great Park. By 1931 Thelma's affair with the prince had been going on for a year, as her marriage to Lord Furness had soured. Gloria remembers spending time at her aunt's house as well as Fort Belvedere, where she is pictured on the lawn kneeling with the prince and his dogs. Thelma's affair finally came to an end in 1934 when she left for a trip, asking her good friend Wallis Simpson, whom she had introduced to Edward years before, to "look after him while I am away. See that he doesn't get into any mischief."[11]

Young Gloria spent summers in Deauville, Monte Carlo, and Biarritz, where her mother found a villa large enough to accommodate her sister and friends, but not her own daughter and the Caravan. They were put up in a hotel nearby.

OPPOSITE:
Gloria with the Prince of Wales at Burrough Court in Melton Mowbray, near the prince's country house. Burrough Court was the hunting estate of Lord Marmaduke Furness, her aunt Thelma's second husband. Thelma and the prince began an affair in 1930, which lasted until 1934 when she left for a trip and asked her friend Wallis Simpson to look after him. "I would love talking to him when he had breakfast in bed. He was wonderful talking with a child," recalls Gloria. "And he always had those Cairn terriers. Years later, at a subdeb dance at the Waldorf, I rode up in the elevator with him and the duchess. I told him I remembered the terriers, and she said, in the iciest voice, 'Sweet little things, weren't they?'"

The first crack in the Caravan came when Gloria's mother moved the family back to Paris into a house on rue Alfred Roll. Now it seemed there was no room for Naney, who had become increasingly outspoken and difficult with regard to her daughters' social lives. Gloria and Thelma threatened to commit their mother to an insane asylum if she refused to live elsewhere.[12] But the relationship that had pushed Laura Morgan over the edge was Gloria's romance with Prince Friedel Hohenlohe. If they married, she would move to Germany with young Gloria, and Naney would be cut off from the fortune that supported them all. This was a crisis she had to address. She started a campaign to influence her granddaughter to fear her mother. Today Gloria reminisces: "It is no surprise that, along with her prayer book, Naney Morgan kept *Napoleon* by Emil Ludwig at her bedside and read and reread it since 1916. Looking back on it, my adored Naney could well be called Naney Napoleon."

It was during a weekend at Burrough Court that the trouble began, when Gloria was asked to write a letter dictated to her by her nurse, Dodo. The letter was addressed to her grandmother Morgan, and Gloria was told to write that she missed Naney and also to say that "MY MOTHER IS A RARE BEASE." (The word "beast" was dictated misspelled so it would seem childlike.)[13] Dodo cried hysterically as she asked the child she loved to fabricate such a lie. She could not escape this terrible mission, having received orders from Laura Morgan herself, who had a plan that would put an end to the romance with Prince Hohenlohe and, in so doing, would ultimately lead to the trial that would make the future a living hell for her family. She had decided that the time had come for Gloria to meet the Vanderbilt side of her family so she could be taken into the fold.

Gertrude Vanderbilt Whitney was fifty-seven years old when she greeted her eight-year-old niece in 1932. Reggie's sister had heard unsavory reports from Naney about how her brother's widow was living on the Vanderbilt money that was supposed to support Gloria. Her intervention might be needed, but until then, she could get to know her niece, whom she had not seen since Gloria was an infant. Gloria was soon to find that there was nothing cozy or embracing about Aunt Gertrude. She was a formidable, complex woman who had emerged from

OPPOSITE:
Gloria and her beloved nurse, Emma Sullivan Keislich, whom she called "Dodo" and "Big Elephant." Dodo and her grandmother Naney made up what Gloria called "the Caravan." "The Caravan was home to three—Dodo, Naney, and me. It was steamer trunks, packing and unpacking on ocean liners, in hotels, on trains, in rented houses in Paris, Cannes, England—it mattered not where as long as we three were together."

her own trials within the gilded cage of her family and marriage to Harry Payne Whitney. Her marriage in 1896 had taken place in the Gold Room at The Breakers. Harry Whitney was the perfect, dashing millionaire match for a Vanderbilt heiress. Harry's family's immense fortune provided the mansion he grew up in opposite Gertrude's on Fifth Avenue. There was also an 110,000-acre camp in the Adirondacks, an 8,000-acre estate in the Berkshires in New England, and houses in Newport and Old Westbury on Long Island. Gertrude had three children: Flora was born in 1897, Cornelius (Sonny) in 1899, and Barbara in 1903. But Gertrude discovered early on that unless she made her own life, she would suffer the same fate as so many heiress wives whose husbands found their fun and passion outside of the marriage. Thus she cultivated a life in the arts, both as a patron and a sculptor. She founded the Whitney Museum of American Art in 1931, after the Metropolitan Museum of Art turned down her offer of seven hundred American paintings from her collection in 1929.

There were two distinct sides to Gertrude, who lived in splendor in her mansion at 871 Fifth Avenue but increasingly favored her bohemian Greenwich Village studio in the Washington Mews later in life. Widowed in 1930, she provided her grown children and their families houses on her vast Old Westbury estate, complete with tennis courts, riding stables, kitchen and cutting gardens, and her beautiful studio, designed by William Adams Delano in 1912, where she did her sculpture.

Gloria remembers Gertrude as "tall and extremely thin and [having] exquisite taste in the way she presented herself. At Old Westbury she would wear variations of the same look—beautifully cut English slacks with tailored silk shirts, several ropes of pearls and hats (in the house) made of tweed and a jaunty feather tucked in. It was considered eccentric in 1932 for a woman to wear pants, and the first time I met her at Old Westbury I was quite startled, never having seen a woman in pants before. She wore a pair of pearl bracelets (one on each wrist), designed with six strands of pearls clasping a large platinum square, encrusted with a pattern of smaller diamonds surrounding one large round diamond in the center. In her will she left one of these bracelets to me and one to my sister Cathleen with

LEFT:
This painting of Old Westbury, Gloria's
Aunt Gertrude's estate in Long Island, by
Thomas Adrian Fransioli, hangs in her living
room today. The estate was her favorite
of all Gertrude's kingdoms; however, in all
the years she lived there, she never felt at
home; the bedroom that was designated
for Gloria had been Harry Whitney's, and
it was never redecorated to suit a young
girl, but bore her uncle's brown furnishings
the entire time Gloria lived there.

the notation 'my pearl and diamond bracelets which I almost always wear.' And so she did. I never saw her without them, country or city or summering in the Adirondacks."[14]

Getting to really know Aunt Gertrude would be impossible for young Gloria, no matter how generous her invitations were, even in the more relaxed setting of the Whitney camp, where she spent the summer of 1932 while her mother was still in Europe. But Gertrude did provide a new order and stability for Gloria, something she had not experienced in her peripatetic childhood. In the meantime, Laura Morgan had moved to the Hotel Fourteen on East Sixtieth Street in New York City, where she would live from then on. From this command post, she directed a campaign against her daughter as an unfit mother. Gloria knew exactly what was going on when she was told to fake the symptoms of various illnesses for family doctors in an effort to show that her health was endangered by her mother's negligence. Her grandmother's appetite for revenge on her daughter eclipsed the needs and well-being of her granddaughter, who was her only vessel of hope.

When Gloria's mother returned from Europe, she joined Gloria and Dodo in a townhouse at 39 East Seventy-second Street. The rest of the household consisted of the butler, Zaug, and Beesley, the chauffeur of her mother's friend, the financier A. C. Blumenthal. Beesley would be waiting every day in Mr. Blumenthal's Rolls-Royce, ready to take Gloria and Dodo anywhere they wanted to go.[15] This was now home, but the presence of her mother's elder sister, Consuelo, who was hostile to Gloria, cast a long shadow of fear; she was like a snake that might strike at a moment's notice—and strike she did.

One rainy day, Gloria overheard Aunt Consuelo advising her mother that she must "get rid of that nurse, the sooner the better,"[16] and suggesting that they might ask Prince Friedel for his help. That did it. The Caravan was under attack and things had to happen immediately in order to save what was left of it.

The sequence of events that triggered the trial must have seemed like a nightmare for young Gloria. Overhearing her aunt's urging that her beloved Big Elephant be fired, she fled in Blumenthal's waiting car with Dodo to Aunt

60.

OPPOSITE:
Gertrude Vanderbilt Whitney in her sculpture studio with her assistant, Juliana Force, who was also the first director of the Whitney Museum of American Art when it was founded in 1931, located on Eighth Street in Greenwich Village. Gloria says of her aunt: "She appeared old to me and there was a reserve and distance about her that was hard to break through. At Old Westbury, although wearing a hat, I never saw her walk around the grounds or leave the house. She was never there during the week but would drive out from the city on weekends, and until Dodo left, she would prompt me to run down the stairs and hug her ecstatically. Aunt slept late in the mornings and I would hang around waiting for the butler to bring her tray up to Hortense, her personal maid, who would be waiting outside her door to carry it into her room. I wouldn't see her until late afternoon, when she would emerge coiffed and elegant in her usual 'uniform.' Her hair was orange-red and always so perfectly coiffed. I irreverently suspected it might have been a wig? But of this I am not certain."

Gertrude's studio on Eighth Street. There Gloria enacted such a frightening drama that Gertrude truly feared for her health. She led the only people who had the power to save her to believe she was afraid of her mother and didn't want to be in her company ever again. "And it was true—I was, because I was terrified knowing that she had the power to take Dodo, the only mother I had, away from me forever,"[17] Gloria says today.

The trial to determine who would win custody of young Gloria Vanderbilt began October 1, 1934, concluding with Judge John F. Carew's decision on November 21 to award custody to Gertrude Vanderbilt Whitney. The ruling included the provision that Gloria could see her mother for one day each weekend, the entire month of July, and eight hours on Christmas Day. The photographs of the ten-year-old Vanderbilt heiress entering and leaving court are particularly shocking: they show a little girl who is never comforted by a grown-up's arm around her shoulder, or anyone holding her hand. Instead she is always walking alongside her Aunt Gertrude, or a lawyer, or a grim-faced detective.

Gloria says, "There was a period before the court decision came down when I was desperately preoccupied with my father, and to this day I remember the shame I felt at the blustering retort of 'Certainly not!' when, during one of my sessions with Frank Crocker [Gertrude Whitney's lawyer], I got up the courage to ask him, 'Would you be my father?'"[18] How much more alone could a young child feel during the most frightening ordeal of her life? But the worst was yet to come. Judge Carew also ruled that the last link of the Caravan be broken. He ordered that Dodo was to be dismissed. Gloria was not to have any contact with her, nor would she know her whereabouts. Dodo was to be replaced by a new governess. It was the final blow.

"The one thing that I wanted was my nurse Dodo to stay with me, and that was not to be," Gloria reflects now. "Dodo took charge of me at the Lying-In Hospital where I was born and was with me until the day she was dismissed by the court. This was the day the happiness of my childhood ended. It was the most terrible thing that had ever happened to me and tore my life apart. Left alone in the alien

DAILY NEWS

The a... for ...

Daily --- 1,550,000
Sunday - 2,400,000

Copyright 1935 by News Syndicate Co., Inc. Reg. U. S. Pat. Off.

NEW YORK'S PICTURE NEWSPAPER

Entered as 2nd class matter, Post Office, New York. N. Y.

Vol. 17. No. 7   40 Pages   New York, Thursday, July 4, 1935★

2 CENTS IN CITY LIMITS

2 Cents IN CITY LIMITS | 3 CENTS Elsewhere

GLORIA LOSES CHILD

Mrs. Harry Payne Whitney and Gloria at fair on her Manhasset estate.

"Thank God they exonerated me of those disgraceful charges," Mrs. Gloria Morgan Vanderbilt (above, leaving dress shop) declared when told of ruling. She insisted she'd continue fight for Gloria.

Story on Page 3

MRS. VANDERBILT CLEARED.—Sustaining Justice Carew's decision in awarding Gloria Vanderbilt to her aunt, Appellate Division yesterday cleared child's mother, Mrs. Gloria Morgan Vanderbilt, of charges brought by former maid. Ruling left way open for child's return to mother at some future time. Mrs. Vanderbilt said she'd carry case to highest court in State.

—Story on page 3.

OPPOSITE:
Gloria during the custody trial, as she was ushered through the crowds into the courtroom

RIGHT:
The media was obsessed, and it was headline news for months.

world of strangers in Old Westbury, with Naney living in New York at the Hotel Fourteen (and Aunt Gertrude coming out only on weekends), my lifeline was a call every night to Naney at 7 PM—VOlunteer 5-6000. I longed for the times [I was] permitted to visit Naney in her dark one-room apartment, which looked over an elevator shaft. Her narrow bed in an alcove—over it hung a black crucifix, and under this a huge calendar on which, as it passed, each day would be blotted out in heavy ink. Naney's only interest was, as she put it, 'my own flesh and blood.' She had no close woman friends, if any friends at all."[19]

The contrast between her beloved Naney's living conditions and the luminous but lonely environment of Old Westbury was striking. "On her windowsill a bottle of milk and on a table nearby, biscuits in a tin box painted with mythical creatures lolling in a forest of snow-covered trees. The milk for Naney's café au lait breakfast, along with hot water spiked with lemons heated on an electric plate. She spent a lot of time poring over the *Wall Street Journal* and on the phone with her broker, but she knew this bored me and during my visits we never wasted our time together over such mundane preoccupations. Every day at four o'clock she sallied forth to Schrafft's around the corner for a solitary dinner. 'Never tip too much,' she would tell me. 'They won't respect you if you do.' (Advice I've never followed.) The room in need of paint, the faded carpet, the colorless frayed upholstery on two comfortable chairs by the fireplace, the darkness of the room, was to me a haven of paradise. The Caravan may no longer have had wheels—and even though Dodo was no longer part of it, I had my Naney and it was home. Later when I became twenty-one and could afford it, I begged her to move into a larger apartment because I thought it would make her happy. Finally she did—three sun-filled rooms with spectacular views—but it was never the same again."[20] Gloria recalls, seventy-six years after the trial.

But these events did not break Gloria. When her happiness ended, a warrior spirit was born.

66.

3.

COMING HOME

*"Everywhere order, and it was perfect. And it lived
with such ease. Is that what luxury meant?"*
—GLORIA VANDERBILT, ONCE UPON A TIME

OPPOSITE:
Gloria at the age of seventeen,
photographed by Horst P. Horst on a visit
back to New York during the summer she
stayed in Beverly Hills with her mother.
She is wearing a dress by Howard Greer,
who was famous for designing what
was then known as a "tabletop" dress,
which looked good from the waist up
when stars were photographed sitting
in restaurants and nightclubs. The ring
is by Paul Flato. In Horst's book *Salute
to the Thirties*, Valentine Lawford wrote
of Gloria's portrait, "This photograph
(taken after the thirties) is included.
Horst considers Gloria Vanderbilt one
of the most original and attractive
American women he has ever known."

With the trial behind her, Gloria found herself back at Aunt Gertrude's estate in Old Westbury. She was enrolled in the Greenvale School in Glen Head on Long Island, with a strict regime monitored by her new governess, Mademoiselle Ruel. Her austere aunt was still elegant, but now with just the faintest trace of caricature, sporting ever-present pearls beneath a series of feathered hats—even indoors. Gloria notes she wore "white silk shirts always, never colors. Around her waist a black crocodile belt looped around the pants, and high-heeled black crocodile shoes. The effect of her torso appeared without curves, possibly androgynous, a model's figure made for beautiful clothes. It would be inconceivable to imagine her naked. There was also something wonderfully theatrical about her, the face somewhat masklike (not very good skin), something about her stagey, like

a character in Grand Guignol. I did not think she was beautiful, but these other things about her fascinated me. And of course everyone around her treated her as a Queen Bee and that kind of power to a child is unquestioned."[1]

Gertrude did what she could to make her niece feel at home, but this did not include redecorating Gloria's new bedroom. It had belonged to her late husband, Harry Whitney, and the somber palette of brown curtains, rug, and leather upholstery remained intact for the seven years Gloria stayed there. Gertrude also never, ever communicated with her niece directly. Gloria remembers: "She did so through the intermediary of one of her lawyers, the dreaded Frank Crocker, who had told me that Dodo was leaving and I would never see her again. The other lawyer, who stood in for Crocker sometimes, was Thomas Gilchrist, appointed by Judge Foley as my legal guardian. I found this confusing and dreaded the times I was told they were coming to 'talk to me.'"[2]

Nevertheless, Gloria loved Old Westbury the most of all Gertrude's residences, as she felt that the New York City mansion at 871 Fifth Avenue had, as one of her friends had suggested, the coziness of Grand Central Terminal. There was order and calm everywhere, in contrast to the rented houses and hotel rooms that Gloria had lived in as a child in Europe. Gertrude's devoted staff was headed up by her personal maid, Hortense, and her butler, William, who stood at attention behind Gertrude's chair during meals ready to decipher the slightest flick of a finger, signaling whether she wanted the next course or seconds. The house had an atmosphere of quiet sensuality, with bowls of fragrant potpourri and vases brimming with fresh flowers everywhere. Yet as welcome as this calm might have appeared, still today Gloria remembers that "from the day I went to live with Gertrude to the day I left, I always felt an imposter, a changeling there under false pretenses—never welcomed by Gertrude's children who had houses on her estate. The only place I felt I belonged was when with Dodo and Naney."[3]

As a teenager, Gloria was given the chance to decorate a small room in a building called the Cottage, which connected to the main house by a passageway. She chose an Egyptian theme, and converted the room into a dazzling den of color and printed textiles where she could entertain her friends and serve them Turkish coffee. She found incense to burn that added "just the right touch." She called it "exotic but American cozy."[4] The décor and her description of this very first project were prophetic, the beginning of Gloria's talent for expressing her own indelible sense of style. But the seemingly charmed life she led in her aunt's

71.

OPPOSITE:
Gloria and Aunt Gertrude perched on their Louis Vuitton steamer trunks. They had just returned from a vacation in Cuba, where Gloria visited her half-sister Cathleen.

OPPOSITE:
The grand sixty-foot ballroom at 871 Fifth
Avenue, where Gertrude had planned to
give Gloria her coming-out party before
fate intervened. Stanford White, famous
for importing great treasure from European
palaces and installing suites of rooms in his
mansions, gilded the room with boiserie
originally from a château in France that
belonged to one of Louis XIV's courtiers.

cloistered domain could not obliterate the outside world. Her first visit with her mother during the summer of 1935 was relentlessly chronicled by paparazzi, who were staked out to record her every move from vantage points in the bushes and in boats offshore of her mother's rented summerhouse. A childhood friend of Gloria's, Diane Meredith Volz, recently unearthed a box of seventy-year-old newspaper clippings. They bring to life the full horror of what it must have been like for Gloria to have her every move publicly scrutinized, as guards with machine guns silently patrolled everywhere she went that summer.

Gloria's resilience was strengthened as she took refuge in her creativity and the world she was discovering. She delighted in visits with her grandmother Morgan at the Hotel Fourteen, intrigued by her whimsical, magpie décor. She spent hours during her visits drawing imaginary houses, creating a fantasy of the world where she would move her Caravan when she was finally grown up. She reveled in the magic of her aunt's other life near Washington Square in Greenwich Village. Gertrude founded the Whitney Museum of American Art in 1931 in a series of buildings that she converted on Eighth Street, and she also owned a little house made up of former stable buildings at 60 Washington Mews. Gloria discovered a new kingdom of beauty. She writes of her bedroom in the Mews: "I fell in

ABOVE:
The judge had ruled that Gloria was allowed to see her mother one day on the weekends, the entire month of July, and eight hours on Christmas Day after her aunt won the custody trial. The outings were accompanied by the governess of the moment. Here she remembers "more horror, utter bewilderment, and panic" in this photograph with her mother "and one of the many Dodo replacements."

OPPOSITE:
A photograph from a home movie that was made during the summer of 1935, when Gloria stayed with her mother in a house she rented in Smithtown on Long Island. "All I wanted was to go to the movies," Gloria remembers, "so Aunt Thelma said, 'Why don't we make one of our own!'" Here she is with her mother and her cousin Tony Furness, who was there with his mother.

MISS GLORIA VANDERBILT—She emerges at fifteen, inevitably the next glamour girl. She is not out, but she is already a personality. Her Javanese beauty distinguishes her from her curly-headed contemporaries. Her tastes are definite. At the moment she is interested in things Egyptian. She wears a curious Egyptian bug ring on her hand and she has designed her own Egyptian room in her aunt's house. She was photographed for Harper's Bazaar on Mrs. Harry Payne Whitney's lawn on Long Island.

love with this room and forever tried to recapture it, but it was hard to define and has always eluded me. It had to do with the two French doors looking out onto the snow falling on the empty cobblestoned street below, framed by curtains of taffeta of palest lavender spilling from the ceiling onto the floor in pools of silk and rustling across the windows at dusk in a most seductive way."[5]

Gertrude's assistant, Juliana Force, who became the Whitney's first director, lived on the top floor of the museum building. True to her name, she became a source of support and encouragement for Gloria, providing her with the first real glimmer of positive reinforcement. During one visit, Gloria dared to ask Juliana if she might speak with Gertrude about allowing Gloria to have visits with her mother that were less regulated. She loved Juliana's unconventional decorating—especially a floor strewn with a pattern of vibrant flowers, which turned out to be printed fabric that she had shellacked over and over again to create her own primrose path. Chairs were covered in pink velvet and lemon-yellow satin. They took tea from a cart heaped with plates of delicacies. In this resplendent atmosphere Juliana gained Gloria's confidence, assuring her that she would talk to her aunt, and that her request would be granted. Sure enough, it was. Judge Foley gave permission for spontaneous visits from then on. The door had been opened, and this new sense of confidence made other small miracles possible. Gloria's grandmother not only told Gloria where Dodo was, but she was allowed to go and see her beloved nurse! This was just the beginning.

The world was opening up for young Gloria, who was growing into her unusual beauty. She had gone from Greenvale to Miss Porter's School in Farmington, Connecticut, and then on to the Mary C. Wheeler School in Providence, Rhode

OPPOSITE:
A star is born. Louise Dahl-Wolfe took the first photograph of Gloria for *Harper's Bazaar* when she was fifteen years old, after Diana Vreeland, then the editor of the fashion magazine, had seen Gloria at her aunt's house at Old Westbury. "This was the first time I had even heard of the pancake makeup the stylist patted on my face—I was thrilled!" She wore a tufted red leather heart pin, all the rage at the time. "I was so enamored of that pin," she says. "It was one of my favorites." She was also fascinated by all things Egyptian at the time, and at just fifteen years old had already designed her own Egyptian-themed room at the house.

ABOVE LEFT:
Gloria at one of the many juniors dances she attended in New York City

ABOVE RIGHT:
Gloria at the Mary C. Wheeler School in Providence, Rhode Island

ABOVE & OPPOSITE:
André Kertész photographed Juliana Force's checkerboard door and apartment for the October 1947 issue of *House & Garden*. Juliana befriended Gloria, earning her trust, and would invite her for tea in her exotic living room. The floral pattern on the floor, accomplished with many coats of lacquer over fabric, was to inspire Gloria's own decorating in later years. "She was simply amazing," Gloria remembers. "She just knocked my socks off."

BELOW:

The house at 719 North Maple Drive in Beverly Hills, rented by Gloria's mother and Aunt Thelma. It was here, during a 1941 visit on a summer break from school, that Gloria's life changed forever. "That is where I met Howard Hughes," she says, pointing to the front door. "He called my mother saying he wanted to come and talk to her. And she thought he was interested in her. As he was arriving, I was going out the door, and we met briefly. He asked my mother permission for me to take a screen test, and later we went out on a date."

Island, where she made wonderful friends and felt truly happy. She also had an art teacher who was supportive of her talent. And there were boys, Johnny Delahanty and Geoffrey Montgomery Talbot Jones, and there were dances. There were more palaces and kingdoms to explore. She went on a trip to California with her mother when she was thirteen, and they were guests at William Randolph Hearst's castle in San Simeon. She went to Cuba to visit her half-sister, Cathleen, who was about to marry Martin de Arostigui.

There were tea dances at the Plaza and subdebutante dances, which necessitated buying evening dresses and wearing makeup and pleading with Gertrude to relent on having Gloria's every move chaperoned. There was a succession of governesses, all dreadful, with the exception of the lovely Kate Drury, in whom Gloria could actually confide.[6] She met Carol Marcus at Old Westbury when Geoffrey Jones and his Princeton friends brought her out to visit one day. Gloria, Carol, and Oona O'Neill, whom Gloria met around this time at a subdebutante ball, became lifelong friends.

And then there was the appendectomy that melted away any trace of baby fat, leaving Gloria with a willowy figure to rival any starlet's—not that she quite believed it yet. Diana Vreeland, then fashion editor of *Harper's Bazaar*, came to visit Gertrude at Old Westbury. Gloria showed her Egyptian room to Vreeland, who loved it. Days later, Vreeland called Gertrude to ask permission for Gloria to be photographed by Louise Dahl-Wolfe for the magazine. Gloria was in heaven; she took to being photographed "the way a duck takes to water."[7] She was fifteen years old. Gertrude was already talking about the coming-out party she planned to throw at 871 Fifth Avenue when Gloria graduated from Wheeler. But that was far off in the distance, an eternity away.

The summer of 1941 arrived with a special adventure for Gloria. During summer break at the end of June, she went to California to visit her mother, who had taken a house at 719 North Maple Drive in Beverly Hills with Thelma and her twelve-year-old son, Tony. Never mind that Gloria was chaperoned by her governess, Constance, and never mind that when she arrived at the airport in Los Angeles her mother wasn't there to meet her—they hadn't seen each other

OPPOSITE:
George Hurrell, photographer to
the Hollywood stars, photographed
Gloria—trying to look much older than
her age, seventeen—during the summer
of 1941. She found the bracelet, made of
clamshells strung on elastic, in Santa Monica.

ABOVE:
"Oh, Mocambo," Gloria says, smiling at
the memory of her first visit to the famed
nightclub. "It was *the* place where all the
stars would go on Saturday night. And I
was so starstruck. All the men dressed in
black, and the women would appear in the
most beautiful gowns. I remember Dorothy
Lamour was dating a bigshot lawyer, and
they got into an argument. I don't think
anyone noticed but me. She started crying,
and I just remember thinking I was privy to
some amazing moment in their romance. The
next week he was there with Alice Faye."

since Christmas. And no surprise that when she finally got to the house later that
morning, her mother was still asleep, as was Thelma. There was no one to greet
her, except, of course, Wannsie, her mother's loyal personal maid.

Days after her arrival her mother threw a party for Gloria. All of a sudden, the
movie stars she had seen on the big screen came to life right in front of her, and
not only that, they were asking her out. Geoffrey Jones, back in New York, now
seemed a "callow youth," replaced by grown-up men with names like Van Heflin,
Errol Flynn, and George Montgomery.[8] The duck that had taken to water gave way
to a bird that flew out of its cage, and the sky was the limit.

That summer, Hollywood was a luscious playground teeming with gorgeous
movie stars, who filled their evenings dining and dancing at nightclubs like Ciro's,
Romanoff's, and the Mocambo. Gloria was a new flame for all the handsome
moths vying for her attention. Good-bye, Old Westbury with Constance monitor-
ing her every move! Good-bye, tea dances at the Plaza and subdebutante dances
at the Waldorf! Hollywood was seething with sophistication and glamour, a heady
dreamscape that she could enter without a chaperone. Her mother didn't ask
whom she was seeing, what she was doing, or where she was going from one day

to the next. Constonce was sent back to Gertrude's, leaving Gloria to navigate this glittering terrain on her own. Meanwhile her mother was involved in a relationship with an actress named Kitty Kelly, who lurked in the background and contributed to the elder Gloria's often dazed behavior, while Thelma was busy with her romance with the actor Edmund Lowe, who often stayed over at the house. There were a lot of closed doors and empty mornings, except for Wannsie's presence bringing order to the haze.

Gloria had suitors galore. Van Heflin even proposed marriage, but that soon went up in smoke and he was replaced by many others, including Phil Kellogg, who had met Gloria on her first trip out West with her mother at the age of thirteen. Phil took her on a date to swim at the Beverly Hills Hotel pool, where she wore a hot pink bathing suit.[9] There she met a new suitor. His name was Pasquale "Pat" De Cicco, and he loomed like a black cloud, blotting out the sun for Gloria. He traveled with a pack of regulars: fun-loving, gambling Hollywood players like Joe Schenk, the head of Twentieth Century Fox; the actor Bruce Cabot; and the agent Charlie Feldman,[10] who made it their business to light up a party with gags and stories. De Cicco worked for Howard Hughes; some said as a talent scout, but no one ever really knew exactly what he did. He was handsome in a slick sort of way, with dark hair and an even darker personality. His temper might flare up for an instant in company, but you weren't privy to the full force of the gale unless you had the misfortune to marry him. Pat's first wife, the actress Thelma Todd, had been murdered in 1935. The crime remains unsolved to this day, but the whispered speculation was that her volatile husband knew the answer to the mystery, if in fact he wasn't *the* answer.

Pat made Gloria uneasy, yet she was susceptible to him, especially because he played the game of hot-and-cold with her. This threw her off her newly discovered powers; he was the one she wasn't sure of, he was the one who risked making her jealous. The other men who came courting didn't play those games, and like so many people around Gloria, Pat had a plan for her. She might have escaped it, if things had worked out differently with Pat's boss.

One day Gloria's mother snapped out of her haze, buzzing with excitement because Howard Hughes had called to say he wanted to see her. There was a great fuss about what she would wear, and then the thrill of trying to imagine what he wanted to discuss when he came to the house. Upon learning that his mission was to ask if she would allow him to give Gloria, whom he hadn't met, a screen test,

LEFT:

Gloria with the actor George Montgomery and actress Cobina Wright Jr. "I was dating George and he invited me to the premiere of *Charley's Aunt*, but the studio had paired him with Cobina, so we all showed up together. But guess who went with him to Mocambo?" A newspaper caption of the pair that evening read, "Miss Vanderbilt is causing quite a stir in filmland society."

PAGE 88:

Gloria with Bruce Cabot and Rita Hayworth at El Morocco. "Rita was in New York doing a spread for *Look* magazine, and she had to wear the same clothing for four days so the photos would look like they were all taken the same day," Gloria says.

PAGE 89:

Gloria at El Morocco with Pat De Cicco

PAGES 90 & 91:

Salvador Dalí with Gloria at his Surrealist Ball in 1941, and the invitation to the ball, designed by Dalí

"EL MOROCCO"

the haze descended again in an instant and the door to her bedroom was shut tight. When Gloria asked her advice about whether to accept the offer, her mother snapped, unable to rise above her own feelings of jealousy and disappointment. "Some people shouldn't have children and she really wasn't prepared to have children," Gloria says today of her mother. "Every chance she had to connect with me, she blew it. She really blew it."

By the time the thirty-six-year-old Howard Hughes started courting Gloria, he was well established as a movie producer, aviation engineer, and pilot. He owned Hughes Aircraft and in 1937 had flown in record time cross-country from Los Angeles to New York City. In 1938, he had flown around the world, again setting a record. He was a lanky, mysterious, divorced millionaire who had dated a galaxy of Hollywood stars, including Katharine Hepburn and Ava Gardner.

Gloria gives a delicious description of preparing for her first date with Hughes in *It Seemed Important at the Time*. One can't help but notice the similarities between this moment and her observations as a young girl of her mother's languid routine dressing for evenings out in Paris. She describes soaking in a luxurious milk bath and sipping a cocktail of Dry Sack sherry, served in a frosted silver glass by Wannsie, who also prepared her outfit. She ended up wearing a Lanz of Salzburg peasant skirt and blouse that she says "made me look too young."[11] Perhaps that was because she *was* so young, but she was also beautiful in a startlingly original way.

Hughes swept Gloria off her feet, flying her in his private plane, just the two of them up in the clouds away from everything and everyone—including Pat, who had gotten wind of the romance and couldn't contain himself, issuing a barrage of threats and calling her "Fatsy Roo" and "Stupido," the ugliness of his temper in full swing. It didn't stop Gloria from seeing Hughes, who had Pat sent off on an invented mission to Kansas City just to get him out of Los Angeles and away from Gloria.

Meanwhile, back in New York, Gertrude had had just about enough. Gloria had stayed far past her vacation, had sent her governess home, and was turning Hollywood on its ear. Gertrude's lawyer, Frank Crocker, and Judge Foley summoned Gloria back to Old Westbury. Gertrude had an idea that she thought would lure her niece back into the fold: Gloria could marry her first love, Geoffrey Jones. Once she had put out that bait, Gertrude invited Jones to come out to Old Westbury so Gloria could see him again. She told Gloria that she could have any kind of wedding she wanted. Wouldn't that be nice? Not at all. Gloria told her aunt that she was in love with Howard Hughes, who wanted to marry her. Gertrude quietly made a call to Hughes. Gloria never found out what was said

BELOW:
Gloria's wedding to Pasquale "Pat" De Cicco on December 28, 1941, in Santa Barbara, California. The ceremony lasted four hours. Gloria's mother sold her father's champion horse trophies to help pay for the marriage and planned it to the last detail. "It was a nightmare," remembers Gloria. Members of the wedding party included Betsy Bloomingdale on the far left, Errol Flynn to the left of Gloria, and Carol Marcus at the far right.

in that conversation, but at that moment she knew she had to get away from Gertrude. This decision cost her her relationship with Gertrude, whose parting words to Gloria were: "You just love publicity, don't you! All the publicity you get in Hollywood—you just love all that, don't you!"[12] Gloria remembers vividly today, "I was stunned by the sarcasm in her voice, the bitter hostility in which she regarded me, and was speechless to respond."[13]

They were all gone. Hughes had disappeared, and now that her aunt had dismissed her in that cool rage, how could she go back to Wheeler and finish her senior year? Her mother was wrapped up with Kelly, who seemed to bring out the worst in her, and any hope of reestablishing a connection with her was lost. There was one person, though, who was waiting for her with his plan, and that was Pat De Cicco. Her mother encouraged that plan. Gloria accepted his marriage proposal.

"*Why did I marry Pat De Cicco?* I ask myself today. With hindsight the answer is clear," Gloria says. "That summer of 1941, living in my mother's house on Maple Drive had been like living alone in a hotel. It seemed heaven for a seventeen-year-old girl to be let loose suddenly in Hollywood of all places, after the chaperoned life with Aunt Gertrude at Old Westbury. I could come and go as I pleased without questions from anyone. No one gave a damn. What could be better? Until, as the weeks passed with no one to talk to about the momentous things happening in my young life, the situation at 'the hotel' was becoming a nightmare because of my mother's attachment to Kitty Kelly and their drinking. Kitty was either at Maple Drive or my mother spent nights at Kitty's. They often made calls to me in the middle of the night, saying they heard I was smoking marijuana (not true). Even Aunt Thelma, preoccupied with her lover, came to me saying, 'I don't know what I am going to do about your mother and Kitty!'

"What indeed? Certainly I didn't know. All I knew was that I wanted to get out, away, anywhere. It did occur to me to go back to Aunt Gertrude, but I quickly rejected that idea as her disapproval and hostility the last time we met made it inconceivable. To get married, and fast, seemed the only answer. When I told my dazed mother and my altogether-with-it Aunt Thelma about this, they jumped on

it. What better way of an opportunity—they had been itching for this for years—to tell Aunt Gertrude to go to hell, knowing at seventeen I would need my mother's permission to get married. Fuzzily my mother said, 'Oh Pooks, why, I got married at that age, too,' with Aunt Thelma joining in, 'We'll plan a big wedding—the sooner the better.' I did not realize then that they were 'delighted' I was marrying this possibly dangerous person because suddenly now my mother held all the cards to really tell Aunt Gertrude to go to hell. She may have won her custody case, but now my mother had won the game."[14]

Gloria and Pat were married December 28, 1941. The wedding took place at the Old Mission in Santa Barbara, a Roman Catholic High Mass with all the trimmings, and then a reception back at her mother's house on Maple Drive. The wedding was paid for with the proceeds from the sale of all of Reggie Vanderbilt's horse trophies, as well as the family silver. Judge Foley had the presence of mind to buy it up and gave it back to Gloria years later.

Gloria was an exquisite bride, in a mountain of white satin and tulle with a thirty-foot train trailing behind her. Her mother wore her own wedding dress to the ceremony and reception. Gloria remembers: "When I married De Cicco I walked up the aisle *alone*, as my uncle Harry [Morgan, living in Los Angeles at the time], who would have been the obvious choice to walk by my side, refused. He and his family did not attend the wedding, nor did my Aunt Consuelo. He did not send good wishes, or acknowledge it in any way, as my grandmother (his mother) and Dodo were attending the wedding. My mother said it would not be appropriate for her to walk by my side, so up I went solo. After the endless ceremony, after the priest had pronounced us man and wife, Pat chose not to kiss the bride, and together we walked back down the aisle on the road leading to nowhere. All during the four-hour mass my mind was racing. I thought, 'I can run, I can get out of this!' But I didn't have Howard to run to, only Aunt Gertrude. Years later when I saw that scene in *The Graduate* when Benjamin is screaming for Elaine, and she escapes and runs to him from the altar, I thought: 'If only I had done that!'"[15]

OPPOSITE:
Gloria and her new husband after the ceremony. As to why she married at just seventeen, Gloria says it was an escape. "I always felt like I was an imposter; living with people to whom I was related, but feeling like I didn't belong. I could no longer live with my mother. I could no longer go back to living with Aunt Gertrude. I just wanted to get out, but was too pressured to know I had choices." She quickly discovered that life with De Cicco was not the solution; they were divorced within a few years.

The Weddi

ON THE STEPS of Santa Barbara's historic mission, in which they were wed at high noon yesterday, stand Gloria Laura Morgan Vanderbilt, 17-year-old daughter of a ⫴ wealthy and famous family, a "Pat" Di Cicco, 32. Crowding famed church were hundreds o

OPPOSITE:
The wedding was a major media event.

g of a Vanderbilt

er husband, Pasquale
t the entrance of the
siders—there were but

two score relatives and friends invited—who wanted to
see the heiress and the man she married, an actor's agent
in Hollywood. Following the ceremony a reception was

held in the Beverly Hills home of the bride's mother,
where society and filmland tendered congratulations in a
gay gathering. They plan a honeymoon in Palm Beach.

4.
BUILDING NEW KINGDOMS

"The rooms that wait for us ... rooms we don't know exist yet, but they do."
—GLORIA VANDERBILT, *ONCE UPON A TIME*

Gloria had done the one thing she thought would usher her into the magic kingdom of the Grown-Ups, where she would have control. She was Mrs. Pat De Cicco—and yet nothing had changed. Things seemed to be getting worse. Pat's violent temper and his real occupation, which appeared to be playing cards with the boys, just gathered momentum, beginning on their honeymoon. The newlyweds planned to drive cross-country to Florida to stay at the Everglades Club in Palm Beach—a wedding present from Charles Wrightsman. Gloria recalls that her misery during the ceremony was "topped by the wedding night, spent at Joe Schenk's Palm Springs house, where De Cicco gambled with his chums until 5 AM

as I lay in bed waiting for him. After the wedding night we proceeded on to the endless drive, stopping each night at a motel where I would stand watching as he inevitably registered us as 'Pasquale De Cicco and wife.'"[1]

The war was on, and after their honeymoon at the Everglades Club in Palm Beach, Pat took his bride to Junction City, Kansas, where he enlisted for army training at Fort Riley.[2] Gloria's very first home was a modest two-story cottage near the base. Pat was away at camp during the week, and Gloria had the peace of his absence, now filled by Dodo, who came out to keep her company, as well as Pat's niece, Frances, who understood exactly what Gloria was going through. Gene Tierney and Oleg Cassini, who was also in training at the base, were their neighbors. Tierney was pregnant; Pat had told Gloria *after* they were married that he was unable to have children.

The house was nothing like anything she had ever lived in, but she took pride in fixing it up. She painted the orange-crate night tables a high-gloss white, and the wood barrels that made up the base of their plywood dining table green. It was home, and it was hers to do with as she pleased. Gloria continued to paint

ABOVE:
Gloria and Pat during a trip to New York

OPPOSITE:
Gloria sunbathing in the backyard of the house in Junction City, Kansas, where she and Pat lived while he was in army training the first year of their marriage. Pat's niece came to visit and took this picture with a Brownie camera.

on canvas, too. She had been painting since she was ten years old, but since Pat had taken to calling her "Fatsy Roo van Gogh," she kept her supplies and artwork out of sight.

In photographs, Gloria looks more like a fresh-faced schoolgirl on vacation than a young army wife making her first home. But when Pat was home, it was not a happy household. Soon there were visits to the doctor. Gloria was too ashamed to tell the truth about the cause of her black eyes. It was on a trip to New York, while they were staying at the Pierre Hotel, that the violence got out of hand. Pat's rages were usually freak storms out of nowhere, but a fight at the Copacabana with his nemesis, Harry Cohn, had triggered this particular incident.[3] When they returned to the hotel, he was still furious and pummeled his wife until she blacked out. The next morning Gloria tried to get away, fleeing to the office of her legal guardian, Thomas Gilchrist, who put in a call to Gertrude. Her aunt's attitude was, essentially, "I told you so."

Gloria left Gilchrist's office and called her doctor from the street, but instead of going to see him, she called her husband back at the hotel. He answered the phone wailing like a baby. He had just received the news that his mother had died, and he needed her to come back. But when he saw her, his sense of denial was such that he told her she had better clean up her face. The fact that he had beaten her to a pulp never even crossed his mind. He told her it was "the badness coming out in you, that's it, that's why you look like you do."[4] Gloria returned to him and continued her life as an army wife in Junction City. Not long after her return, she received a message to call Gilchrist. It was never good news when she had to call Gilchrist. He told her that Aunt Gertrude had died. She was only sixty-four. The funeral was to be in New York City at Saint Bartholomew's Church, following a viewing of the body at 60 Washington Mews. Pat went with her to New York but opted to join a card game rather than accompany Gloria to the service.

The time had come for Pat to be shipped overseas for duty, but Gloria's chance to see what life would be like without him was thwarted. He was admitted to the hospital in New York with a potentially fatal case of septicemia, which the doctors were treating with a new drug called penicillin. While Pat was ill, Gloria learned that her half-sister, Cathleen, had died in Cuba. There was so much loss to bear. But Pat recovered, bouncing back better than ever and earning an honorable discharge from the army. Gloria and Pat stayed in New York and rented a

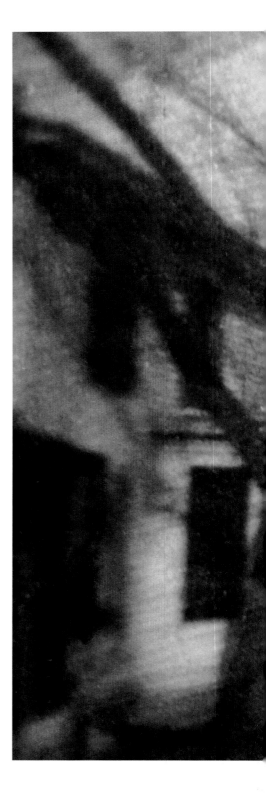

duplex apartment overlooking the East River from her cousin Cornelius "Sonny" Whitney. This was the first of many homes for Gloria with views over the river.

The first act of Gloria's liberation came in February 1945, on the eve of her twenty-first birthday. It was her secret; Pat was not to know. Gloria rented a studio on East Fifty-third Street that had belonged to the French artist Bernard Lamotte. Lamotte, who would later paint the murals for the legendary New York restaurant La Côte Basque, was a dashing bon vivant, and the studio, with its fireplace, kitchen, and roof terrace, had been the scene of many happy gatherings where he cooked and entertained. After classes at the Art Students League on Fifty-seventh Street, Gloria would head back to the studio to paint every afternoon. The war was still going on, and Gloria's best friend, Carol Marcus, had married the writer William Saroyan, who was about to be sent overseas. She and Carol spent days and evenings together as they had as carefree schoolgirls. They were a striking pair, bookends to each other's beauty. Gloria could almost forget that she was married.

Then it happened. One night in early 1945, Gloria and Carol went to a party, and in an instant, the bird flew out of its cage again. The fact that the bird flew into another cage would not be realized for a long time. Gloria met sixty-two-year-old

ABOVE:
Gloria and Carol Marcus, who were best friends along with Oona O'Neill, who eventually married Charlie Chaplin. Carol married the writer William Saroyan twice before she wed actor Walter Matthau. Carol and Gloria were close friends of Truman Capote in the 1940s and early 1950s, and they served as inspiration for Holly Golightly in his novella *Breakfast at Tiffany's*.

OPPOSITE:
Gloria is photographed at Aunt Gertrude's funeral. "Without De Cicco at my side I alone went to the funeral. Cousin Anne and Bill offered to take me back to the hotel in their car, and once inside, I started sobbing."

ATTENDS FUNERAL—Mrs. Pasquale Di Cicco, the former Gloria Vanderbilt, arrives at church to attend funeral of her aunt, Mrs. Harry Payne Whitney, at New York.

(AP) Wirephoto

conductor Leopold Stokowski, and his gaze hit her like lightning. He had been the lover of Greta Garbo. He also had three daughters by two ex-wives: Sonia, his eldest (who was older than Gloria) by his first wife, Olga Samaroff; then Luba, who had been at the Wheeler School with Gloria; and Sadja by his second wife, Evangeline Johnson. On their first date Gloria was Leopold's guest at a concert he conducted at City Center. Afterward, they went to his house for dinner, just the two of them.

Gloria went to Reno to get her divorce from Pat, wearing the gold wedding ring Leopold had designed for her. Although he had said he never wanted to marry again, falling in love with Gloria changed his mind. Their elopement to Mexico in April 1945 turned into a scene from a black comedy, as the plane that Stokowski chartered crashed after flying over the Sierra Nevada mountains. Gloria writes that she "will never forget how as they walked away from the crash, Stokowski, in command, leaned down, pointing to a flower growing in the desert, asking the pilot, 'What is that beautiful flower?', proof to her of his undaunted spirit."[5] They proceeded to dust themselves off and hitchhike to the judge's office in Calexico. The period following the wedding was bliss for Gloria; she felt she had found peace and security. Leopold was the ultimate protector, validating her feelings of being beautiful and loved. His genius and his confidence rooted him to the earth. He would be her foundation as Gloria moved into his kingdom.

Leopold loved her. She was his "Divine Beloved,"[6] but he was very specific about where and how he wanted to live. He owned houses in California: one, aptly called the Monastery, in Santa Barbara, which was to become their cloister, and another at Beverly Crest Drive that Leopold had designed himself. They spent their time there while he was conducting at the Hollywood Bowl. They kept to themselves; why would he want more? He was rehearsing at the Hollywood Bowl and he had his young, devoted wife, who would make him picnic lunches before she drove him to rehearsals, which she would happily sit through, and at the end of the day, together, they would drive back home. Gloria wrote poetry and painted, and Leopold encouraged this. They were solitary pursuits. Gloria would not have to be far away to do her art, and best of all, she would be in the circle of their world; she would not need to go out. But she did need to go out and explore the larger world. At first that need felt as faint as a baby's heartbeat. She took initial steps, exploring exciting new turf: she started taking acting lessons at Paramount Studios. There was something tantalizing about playing other people, the chance to find bits and pieces of yourself that had gotten lost, or hadn't even been discovered yet.

When the Hollywood Bowl concerts came to a close, Leopold and Gloria drove back to the East Coast in an Airstream trailer rigged out to be their very own traveling hearth. Their marriage would mean becoming something of a nomad again, going from city to city, and hotel room to hotel room, packing and unpacking as

110.

OPPOSITE:
A John Rawlings photograph
of Gloria in 1942

Leopold guest-conducted all over the world. They reached New York City, where Leopold now busied himself preparing to conduct the New York Philharmonic. Gloria's Fifty-third Street studio was too small for all their possessions. It was finally time to find a permanent home.

By now, Gloria had control of her own finances. The day that she turned twenty-one, February 20, 1945, she had taken possession of her inheritance. That day, she was alone, as she always had been when dealing with the milestones in her life. She was also completely unprepared for the responsibilities that came with her fortune. Gloria's friend Nancy Biddle recalls incredulously, "Gloria told me she went into a room with a lot of men in black suits, and there wasn't one Vanderbilt, there wasn't one person. You would have thought that someone from the Vanderbilt family would have been there to help her. Nobody."[7] Gloria does remember one instance when she received a letter from Thomas Gilchrist on her tenth birthday informing her that he would be sending her a five-dollar allowance each month, and it would be a good idea for her to keep track of how she spent it. Beyond that, she was on her own. Gloria's mother, who had been living on an allowance from her daughter, now turned the tables, suggesting that Gloria provide her with a trust fund.[8]

Leopold was not in favor of this. He didn't feel that Gloria should support her mother at all any longer. He took charge, in a way eerily reminiscent of what Gloria's grandmother had done years ago on that awful day at Burrough Court when Dodo dictated the letter Gloria had had to write, saying that her mother was a "RARE BEASE." This time it was Leopold who dictated the letter Gloria wrote to her mother telling her of the final cut. Not only that, but he insisted on holding a press conference to announce the establishment of the Gloria Stokowska and Leopold Stokowski Foundation. At the last minute he decided Gloria would go out and face the photographers and reporters alone.[9] The press had a field day with this, reporting that Gloria's mother had to sell her diamond engagement ring as a result of being cut off.

In 1949 Gloria and Leopold bought a house in Greenwich, Connecticut. "It was a tiny little house," Gloria remembers, "and I painted all the floors all different colors. It was really like a dollhouse. Then I had a studio here, and he built a studio for himself that was made of glass bricks, small. But it was really quite magical."[10] At the same time, Gloria was pregnant with their first child. It soon became clear that they would need a base in New York, where Leopold was conducting, so they bought the south penthouse apartment at 10 Gracie Square in New York City. They moved in right before Leopold Stanislas Stokowski III, known as Stan, was born in 1950. As their family continued to grow, they also acquired a larger house in Greenwich, which Leopold preferred to the city.

Gloria was a trooper, taking baby Stan on tour with Leopold, but packing and unpacking was increasingly taxing, as she was pregnant again. She settled down in

112.

OPPOSITE:
This is the first photograph Richard Avedon took of Gloria, her husband Leopold Stokowski, and their firstborn son, Leopold Stanislas Stokowski III (known as Stan), in his studio in the early 1950s. Gloria had not yet met Avedon when she wrote him a letter asking if he might be interested in taking a portrait of her new family. To her delight, he consented, and thus began their lifelong friendship.

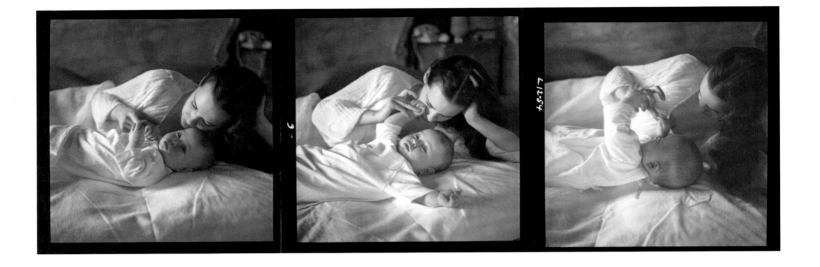

the penthouse at 10 Gracie Square, with Dodo in an adjoining apartment. Her days were quiet as she waited for her next baby. "So I have accomplished much—Dodo has a home, and Naney a room with sunlight," she wrote. "Now if I could only please them in other ways everything would be perfect. Well, one way I do please them, both of them, is Stan. His birth is heralded as a great and real achievement, and rightly so!"[11] Gloria also met a young Irishwoman from Galway who had landed in New York in 1948. Nora Mulkerins was hired to run the household, and has been with Gloria ever since. At eighty-four, and a grandmother of two, she still remains a guiding light who has kept order, running every house for Gloria since the day she arrived more than sixty years ago.

Christopher, Gloria and Leopold's second son, was born in 1952. Gloria kept traveling with her husband, joining him in Toronto and Dallas, then Florence and Rome. She was painting seriously, and in 1952 she had her first one-woman show, at the Bertha Schaefer Gallery. Gloria had rented another studio in the Upper East Side between Fifth and Madison Avenues. Her studios were her private domains, the places where she could be herself and entertain whom she wanted without Leopold's judgment. He looked down on what he called "Vanity Fair" and the superficiality of "Society." He dismissed the fact that Gloria found socializing stimulating and fun.

The one friend of Gloria's in those days who could have been the poster boy for "Vanity Fair" was the writer Truman Capote. He was a frequent guest at the

ABOVE & OPPOSITE:
From a series of photographs that Lillian Bassman took of Gloria and infant Stan at 10 Gracie Square a few weeks after his birth. Gloria had approached photographer Bassman to take the portraits for Leopold Stokowski's birthday.

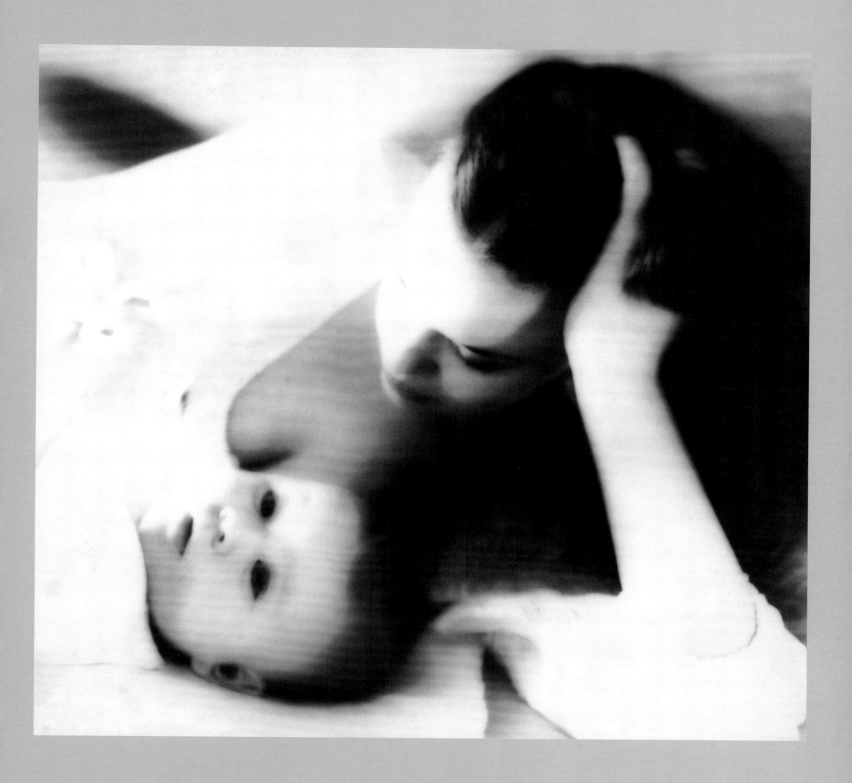

116.

studio, lured by Gloria's social cachet, by her friend Carol Saroyan, who was having a flirtation with the writer Kenneth Tynan, and also by her handsome houseguest, Russell Hurd, who sparked the gregarious writer's fancy. Capote's eavesdropping on Gloria and Carol formed the inspiration for Holly Golightly, the heroine of his novella *Breakfast at Tiffany's*.

The marriage to Leopold had initially felt like Gloria's golden ticket. Here was this brilliant man who loved her and wanted her all to himself. His devotion had put her on a pedestal, but the spotlight would shine only as long as she stayed well within the confined circumference of that circle, and it felt smaller and smaller. In all these years she had not broken through to his inner feelings, and she was wounded that he was unable to open up to her about his past. All her life she had been blanketed by deception from the people she had trusted the most. For an instant she even saw resemblances between Leopold and her grandmother Morgan, something about the way they both withheld things, and were so obsessively possessive.

Leopold traveled so much, and with two small children, she could not accompany him. That faint little drumbeat inside her would not go away. The world outside was waiting, filled with exciting people and so many things she wanted to do.

And there was her mischievous friend Truman Capote, egging her on to start an affair with none other than William Paley, president of CBS. Never mind that Paley's wife, the impossibly gorgeous Babe, was someone that Gloria knew. "Babe knows that he has other girlfriends and she handles it beautifully," was all Capote had to say about the sticky question of infidelity.[12] Gloria didn't have the heart for it.

What she did have the heart for was meeting Marlon Brando after seeing *On the Waterfront*. It so happened that her friend Carol not only knew Brando; she had even been out on dates with him! Gloria was out in Los Angeles before you could count to ten. Brando certainly was anything but the golden ticket, but he did join the legion of famous men who fell at Gloria's feet. The cage door had blown wide open again.

OPPOSITE:
This portrait by Cecil Beaton, taken for *Vogue* in 1953, shows Gloria "with the hairdo that I had when Dick swept it all back, and you see the difference; this is like a wig, almost," Gloria notes, looking at the photograph. The Avedon portrait she is referring to was taken for *Vogue* magazine in the 1950s, and it is also included in Avedon's book *Observations.*

OPPOSITE:

Gloria Vanderbilt, dress by Mainbocher,
New York, March 1955
Photograph by Richard Avedon
for *Harper's Bazaar*

5.

SHOWTIME

*"It may be that the enduring swan glides upon
waters of liquefied lucre; but that cannot account
for the creature herself—her talent, like all talent,
is composed of unpurchasable substances."*
—TRUMAN CAPOTE, *OBSERVATIONS*

Freedom felt like the rush of a waterfall. How could you be blasé when the phone rang and it was your friend, the songwriter Jule Styne, saying that Frank Sinatra wanted to meet you? Frank Sinatra! He was in New York playing at the Copacabana and he had just had a major success with *From Here to Eternity.* Frank Sinatra wanted to meet *you.*

So much more happened in 1954, the year before Gloria got her divorce from Leopold, but she had known that the marriage was over for a long time. She hadn't really wanted to set sail on the *Queen Elizabeth* for yet another tour with Leopold, so when the phone call came that Audrey Hepburn was ill, and could Gloria take

LEFT:
Gloria and Frank Sinatra at the Broadway opening of *Pajama Game* in 1954. Gloria is startled, as paparazzi were not allowed in the theater; they managed to get their shot of the glamorous couple anyway.

April in Paris

B AL S OIE

ABOVE:
The invitation for the "April in Paris" ball in New York in 1954, which Gloria attended when she was asked by the producer Gilbert Miller to fill in for an ailing Audrey Hepburn. Miller was so impressed with her performance (in Hepburn's costume, no less) that he offered her a lead part in his production of Molnar's *The Swan* that summer.

OPPOSITE:
Gloria center stage during the "April in Paris" ball. She is dressed to play John Paul Jones.

over the part in a skit with producer Gilbert Miller at the "April in Paris" charity ball, nothing could stop her. She played John Paul Jones, in Hepburn's costume, to Miller's Benjamin Franklin. The stage was set in more ways than one. Miller was so taken with Gloria that he immediately offered her a role in Franz Molnar's play *The Swan*, which he was producing that summer in Pennsylvania. Gloria played Princess Alexandra, the role that Eva Le Gallienne had originated on Broadway.[1] This was too much "Vanity Fair" for Leopold; he would not attend her stage debut.

Gloria's career in the theater was born. She was proclaimed a star in the making. Miller was quoted as saying that he could "count the stars that I have discovered on the fingers of one hand. There was Ruth Chatterton, Leslie Howard, Audrey Hepburn, and now Gloria Vanderbilt ... she has a running head start in theater—an electric presence, dignity, poise, intelligence, beautiful speech."[2] An August 17, 1954, article in the *New York Herald* trumpeted: "Gloria Vanderbilt a Success in Stage Debut in Poconos." Next came a part in a 1955 revival of William Saroyan's *The Time of Your Life* at City Center in New York. The *New York Journal-American* quoted Gloria: "I'm going to make the stage my career

ABOVE LEFT:
Gloria photographed in 1955 outside City Center, where she was performing in a revival of William Saroyan's *The Time of Your Life*, costarring Franchot Tone.

ABOVE RIGHT:
Gloria in her dressing room, surrounded by flowers and telegrams on opening night of *The Time of Your Life*.

forever."[3] There was a role in NBC's "Kraft Television Theater" in March 1958 and comedy with Art Carney in the "Very Important People" special in December 1959. Bert McCord reported on June 12, 1958, in the *New York Herald Tribune*: "Gloria Vanderbilt will realize a lifelong ambition this summer when she stars in *Peter Pan*." She flew through the air at the Grist Mill Playhouse in Andover, New Jersey. She went back out to Los Angeles in February 1960 to play opposite Gardner McKay in an episode of James Michener's "Adventures in Paradise," a series produced by Dominick Dunne.

The liaison with Sinatra was out in the open, with the press in full court. There is one photograph of Gloria at the theater with Sinatra. She looks like a gorgeous cobra that could kill you with one swift glance. She wrote of Sinatra during this time, "He is the bridge, the bridge to set me free."[4] Clearly he was captivated, as he offered her a part in *Ocean's Eleven*. It was only when she arrived in Hollywood, met not by Sinatra but his chauffeur, and read the script that Gloria realized the movie and the part were not what she had expected. She returned to New York.

This might have come as a blessing in disguise, as Gloria had fallen in love

ABOVE:
Gloria in costume for her theatrical debut,
The Swan. The photo is by Gordon Parks, who
was then working for *Life* magazine, and
with whom Gloria remained lifelong friends.

OPPOSITE:
Caricature of Gloria in *The Swan*
by Al Hirschfeld; the portrait now
hangs in her living room.

with Sidney Lumet, whom she was soon to marry. He was an actor's director; he embodied the true soul of the theater. Everything about Sidney was warm and embracing, and he was Gloria's contemporary—born in 1924. Lumet grew up as a child actor performing in the Yiddish theater. His first marriage, to the actress Rita Gam, ended in divorce in 1955. He had been directing television dramas, and he was on the verge of directing his first film, *12 Angry Men*, when they met. Sidney had also directed Gloria in a summer production of *Picnic* in 1955. (Lumet's directing career includes the films *The Pawnbroker*, *Serpico*, *Dog Day Afternoon*, and *Network*.) Gloria was totally committed to her acting career, taking classes with well-known director and teacher Sanford Meisner at the Neighborhood Playhouse. Her fellow students included Steve McQueen, Joanne Woodward, Marti Stevens, and Peter Falk. The timing couldn't have been more perfect.[5]

Gloria was introduced to Lumet in 1954 by the legendary photographer Richard Avedon. Her friendship with Avedon began in 1952, when, she says, "I took pen in hand and wrote Dick asking if he would take a photograph of me

ABOVE:
Gloria at the Cannes Film Festival with director Sidney Lumet in 1962. They met through Richard Avedon. "Dick thought we were made for each other, and I think it would have worked if I had not been so ambitious. I put my work first. When you are ambitious that way, you don't realize it at the time. I wouldn't do that again. Sidney always put life first and work second."

OPPOSITE:
Gordon Parks photographed Gloria and Sidney Lumet on their wedding day, August 28, 1956.

PAGES 132 & 133:
Richard Avedon took these photographs during a vacation in Round Hill, Jamaica, in 1956 with his family and friends, including Gloria and Sidney. The man disappearing in the water with the chessboard is the writer Cleveland Amory.

with Leopold and [our] infant son Stan. I passionately admired his photographs. Leopold and I led a very reclusive life at the time and it was a huge event for me when he wrote back saying YES. The appointment was made and he said to come wearing 'evening makeup,' which I hadn't a clue about as I wore very little makeup, day or evening. So off we went, carrying Stan. The minute I met Dick I knew (shy as I was in those days) that he was someone I had met before … where or when? It was after that first meeting Diana [Vreeland] called, asking me to pose for *Harper's Bazaar*, no doubt requested by Dick."[6] The call led to Gloria's reappearance in *Harper's Bazaar* for the first time since her magazine debut when she was fifteen.

Their great friendship lasted until Avedon's death in 2004, and it produced an extraordinary archive of personal and professional photographs of Gloria, her family, and their friends. Avedon was to play a pivotal role in Gloria's life in many ways. Gloria recalls their early friendship when "I knew my marriage was over and started to make a new life. When I separated from Leopold, Dick said there was someone he wanted me to meet—Sidney Lumet, because he thought 'each would have something to give the other.' Dick and Evie [Evelyn Franklin, Avedon's second wife] were living in Millicent Rogers's beautiful townhouse on Beekman Place, and they gave a party there for Grace Kelly, which is where I met Sidney. It was love at first sight, and from that night on we were together constantly."[7] Gloria was captivated by the Avedon's sense of style. She writes, "It was the first time I saw that amazing poppy Porthault print on sofa/chairs, and they had the most beautiful glasses for drinks, like flower pots with bottom raised at center … hard to describe … and tissue-thin demitasse cups like black chalk … and cookies from Colette's (out of business now, alas), which were thin and filled with lemon curd or marmalade, never found anywhere since. Leopold always said 'the greatest art of all is the art of living,' and Dick and Evie knew how to do it."[8]

Gloria continued to live at 10 Gracie Square after her divorce from Leopold. It was a constantly evolving decorating adventure that fast became a ravishing mecca for entertaining and family life. When Gloria first moved there with Leopold in the early 1950s, it was decorated primarily with conventional English furniture,

OPPOSITE:
Gloria Vanderbilt, New York, September 1959
Photograph by Richard Avedon

PAGE 136:
Gloria Vanderbilt, dress by Mainbocher, New York, March 1960
Photograph by Richard Avedon

PAGE 137:
This scrapbook page shows different takes working toward the final image that was published in *Harper's Bazaar*. Avedon gave the scrapbook to Gloria as a gift, along with many other photographs over the years.

LEFT:
Avedon spent one day photographing Gloria and her family in the apartment at 10 Gracie Square in 1956. "It was completely Dick's idea to come to the South Penthouse and capture the life Sidney and I had together, and the ambience of our happiness," Gloria says. "He gave us a gift of these prints, as he did of the pictures he took at Round Hill in Jamaica. Only a handful of these pictures were ever published. They were his gift to us for having brought us together." A portrait of Gloria by René Bouché hangs in the entrance hall.

to suit his taste. In time, as Gloria started mining her own sensibility, she took the explorer's route, discovering one-of-a-kind pieces like the huge free-form slab of marble she found in a quarry and carted home, where it ended up as a coffee table with wooden logs as its base. Black and white tiles that looked like patent leather covered the floors, and the furniture and art kept pace with Gloria's elegant, independent, haute bohemian life. In 1956, Avedon spent a day photographing Sidney, Gloria, and her sons. These unusual pictures document her joyous well-being. Gloria describes that day: "In a certain sense those photographs are a confession. Dick caught an atmosphere in those moments that exposed a self not yet formed. He sensed a sheer moment-to-moment sense of being alive."[9]

Gloria's son Stan remembers helping his mother with a decorating project there. "At 10 Gracie we helped her put shells in this bathroom. She put, I guess, plaster—I can't remember what it was—that stayed soft for a while, and you could press the shells into the surface and they would dry. I also remember there was a little door, a little five-foot door at 10 Gracie. I think it had a Romanesque arch into one of the bedrooms. Why was it there? I don't know. It was too small for an adult." The apartment was not just a heavenly retreat for adults. Stan and Chris had their own kingdoms there, too. "My brother and I had this sort of playroom there," Stan says, "and the top floor area, that was really great. In the den next to the big living room, there were bookshelves with a library ladder, and we used to jump—move the ladder strategically to the sofa and jump from the ladder onto the sofa, which was slightly discouraged." Stan also recalls the advent of their first color television. "Early on when Sidney was there, we had one of the first color TV sets, and it was really big and heavy and sat right on the floor, and we used to sit two feet away from it on the carpet."[10]

Photographers couldn't resist the elixir of romance and beauty that Gloria created here. Inge Morath did a series of photographs of Gloria on the roof and inside the apartment, where you see the fantastic eight-foot metal candelabra by Philadelphia craftsman Samuel Yellen, which Gloria painted white. The apartment had the enchantment of a film set by the artist Christian Bérard. It was the perfect setting for Christmas parties and lavish evenings, where everyone from Truman

139.

Capote, Marilyn Monroe, and Sammy Davis Jr. to Cecil Beaton, Isak Dinesen, and Elizabeth Taylor would spend hours after dinner around the piano or talking deep into the night. Stephen Sondheim sang the lyrics to his new musical, *Gypsy*, for Gloria on her birthday in 1959.[11]

As exciting as Gloria's social life was, it was balanced by her seriousness and dedication to her work. As well as roles in the theater and her debut art show in 1952, Gloria published a collection of love poems in 1955, the first of many books. In the long run, acting took a subtle toll on Gloria during the seven years she pursued it. She was well aware that it played on aspects of her character that were vulnerable to insatiable longings, and that no matter how much applause rolled in from the audience, it would not ever be enough to fill that place that had been hollowed out so long ago. There had to be other ways to express her talents and creativity.

Avedon took a portrait of Gloria in 1954 for *Harper's Bazaar*. This photograph was included in his 1959 book *Observations*, a collaboration with Truman Capote. Gloria was featured in a portfolio of famous beauties, now known as the "Swans," as Capote began his essay with a quotation from Patrick Conway's journal, in which he describes "a gathering of swans." Marella Agnelli, Babe Paley, and Vicomtesse Jacqueline de Ribes were fellow Swans. Gloria experienced a turning

OPPOSITE:
Inge Morath took photographs of Gloria in the south penthouse at 10 Gracie Square. She is framed by Yellen candelabra, which she painted white.

ABOVE:
Morath asked Gloria to go up on the rooftop of the building for a series of portraits that day.

point sitting for this portrait. She says, "Although I never thought I was beautiful, the looks I had worked for me. But it was the reflection Dick gave back to me of myself that made me believe in myself. I never told him that, as I felt it a magic mantra that might disappear if put into words. But it is the truth and the gift he gave me. That headshot marks the pivotal moment when I knew at last I could trust myself and that I was free. Dick used to talk about that picture—he said he remembered the day, the moment. I'd come to the sitting with my hair just done in a stylized 'Italian' hairdo much admired at the time, with curls pasted here and there around my face. Dick saw me and took a hairbrush and brushed it through my hair, sweeping it back off my face into a nothing-do. It made all the difference! Later, talking about the photograph, he said he knew something had happened inside me, something different—and, of course, the difference was I was free and unafraid."[12]

Her courage helped her endure yet another custody case in 1959, this time over her sons Stan and Chris when Leopold, without warning, contested the custody agreement of their divorce. Gloria remembers, "Leopold feared flying. He was scheduled for a European concert tour, and on the day he boarded a ship for England, I was walking up Madison Avenue at Seventy-second Street. From across the street I heard a man shouting as he ran towards me, 'Glo-ree-a!' He was a process server, who jammed a paper into my hand, saying, 'Take this!' The papers were suing me for custody of Stan and Chris. It came so unexpectedly, and considering my background, Leopold never thought I would have the guts to fight it. But I did, and when he landed in Europe, he was forced to get on a plane and come back to show up in court. I won this case, and at the time Sidney was shooting Tennessee Williams's *The Fugitive Kind* with Marlon Brando. Sidney told me one morning when he came on the set, the crew had hung on his camera a headline from the *Daily News*—something to the effect that 'Gloria won where her mother failed.'"[13]

6.

VANDERBILT GENES

"There is something inside some Vanderbilts that is as strong as a diamond—it gets the job done. It's something you can fall back on. It's an inner strength. Her art saved her. She could put herself into it and it was a world that she was happy in. She can design anything."

—NANCY BIDDLE, INTERVIEW WITH THE AUTHOR ON JUNE 12, 2009

OPPOSITE:
Gloria has been photographed by almost every legendary photographer of the twentieth century. In this portrait by Francesco Scavullo, she is wearing costume jewelry.

Gloria's irrepressible creativity spawned a galaxy of businesses. Her disciplined work schedule was inviolate. No one could disturb her hours alone in the studio. Her first one-woman art show in 1952 at the Bertha Schaefer Gallery was followed by many others, but her exhibition of collage paintings at the Hammer Galleries in 1968 reached a national audience when Johnny Carson, the host of "The Tonight Show," dedicated an entire hour to Gloria.

Two savvy businessmen saw the TV segment and immediately contacted her about new design ventures. Donald Hall signed Gloria to create a line of Hallmark

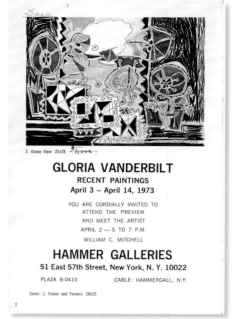

paper products, and Lewis Bloom enlisted her to design fabrics for Bloomcraft. She was the first client of an ambitious, self-made businesswoman, Pearl Bedell, who became Gloria's business agent in the 1970s. In 1970 Gloria was named the design director for Riegel Textile. She was also signed to design dinnerware for Sigma, and in 1973 Gloria was designing bed linens and towels for Martex. Her first foray into fashion was with Glentex, designing scarves. In 1975 *McCall's* had plans to publish a quarterly magazine, simply called *Gloria Vanderbilt*. The idea (long before Martha Stewart) was to empower readers with a how-to spirit, so that they could create their own version of Gloria's enchanted world. The magazine never came to fruition, but *Gloria Vanderbilt Designs for Your Home* was published the same year. In 1976, Seventh Avenue impresario Ben Shaw, who had financed fashion lines by Norman Norell, Geoffrey Beene, and Halston, put up the money for a line of Gloria Vanderbilt dresses. Gloria had become an irresistible magnet. Nobody could get enough of her dazzling, original style.

This burst of creative achievement coincided with Gloria's marriage to Wyatt Cooper. Her marriage to Sidney Lumet ended in 1963, and she married Cooper later that year. Gloria met the writer at a small dinner party given by British actress Leueen MacGrath and her husband, Stephen Goodyear, in their brownstone on East Sixty-second Street. "We were seated next to each other and it was love at first sight. There was the shock of recognition that we would forever after be of utmost importance in each other's lives," Gloria says.[1] They were married on Christmas Eve. If it is said that behind every great man there is a great woman, Gloria and Wyatt Cooper proved the reverse.

146.

ABOVE:
Catalogs from Gloria's shows at the Hammer Galleries. Johnny Carson was so captivated by a show in 1968 that he devoted a segment of "The Tonight Show" to the work, igniting Gloria's career as a designer of home décor and paper products. Soon she would enter the world of fashion design as well.

OPPOSITE:
Gloria's collage painting *The Necklace* (c. 1968) hangs in her living room today.

ABOVE:

Gloria Vanderbilt's artistry and talent spawned multiple business ventures with different design companies in the 1970s. She designed paper products for Hallmark Cards, bed linens for Martex, and became the design director for Riegel Textiles in 1970. Gloria also did home designs for Bloomcraft, and by 1972 she had had fourteen one-woman shows throughout the country. She authored two books on design: *Gloria Vanderbilt Book of Collage* (1970) and *Gloria Vanderbilt Designs for Your Home* (1975). Gloria by Gloria Vanderbilt eyewear for Zyloware is still going strong; she began designing eyeglasses for them in 1976.

OPPOSITE:

A dinner plate design with Gloria's painted flower in a vase produced by Sigma, 1975

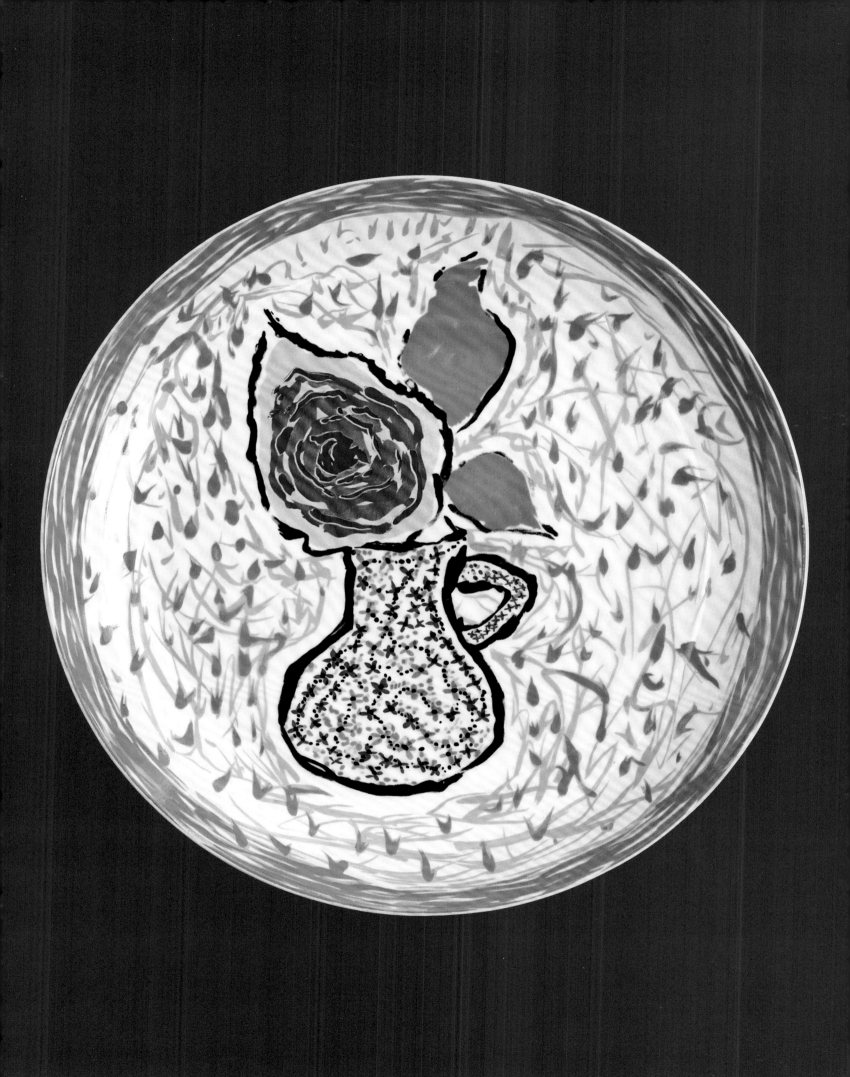

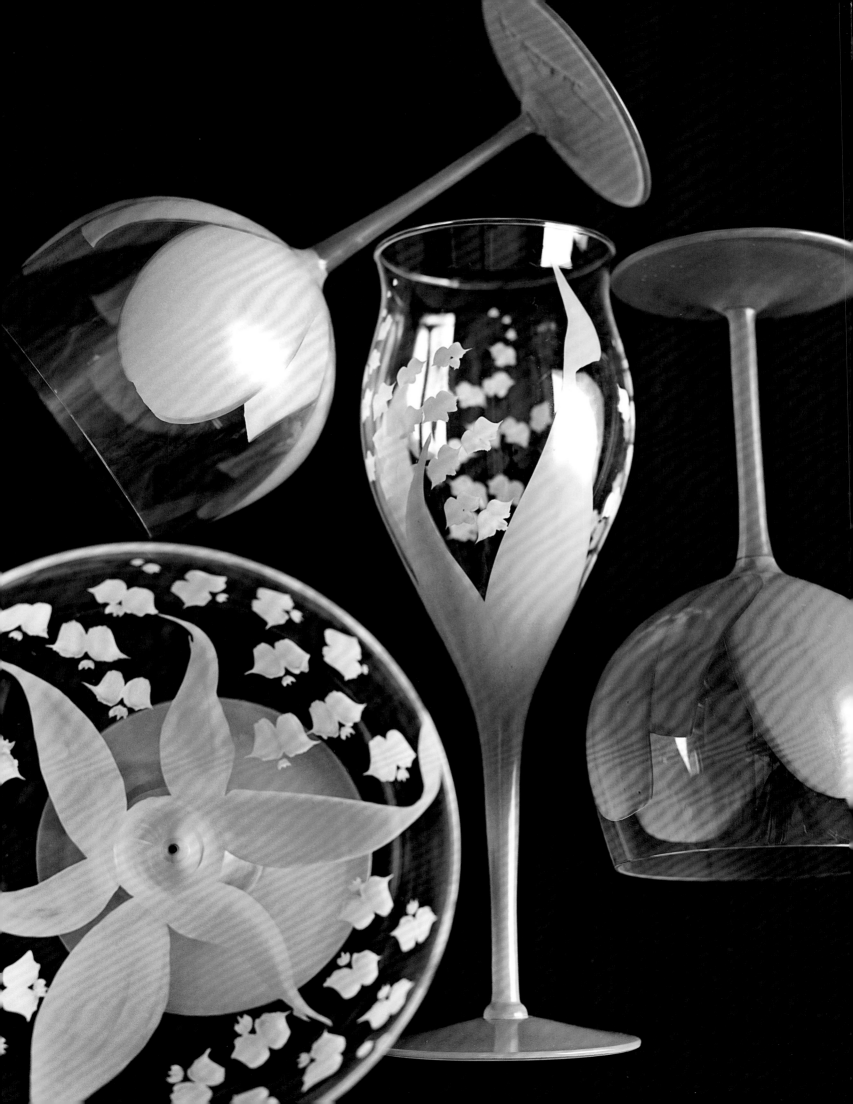

OPPOSITE:
Gloria's stemware design for Sigma with hand-painted flowers of her design

ABOVE:
Horst P. Horst photographed Gloria's country house, Summertime, where she decorated the dining room with her first fabric design for Riegel, a log cabin print.

LEFT:
Two of Gloria's fabric designs for Martex

ABOVE:
Gloria drew crowds wherever she went during public appearances throughout the country.

RIGHT:
Gloria made fashion history, launching the first collection of designer jeans in 1977. Bob Adelman photographed her in the Murjani showroom for the October 14, 1979, issue of the *New York Times Magazine*.

OPPOSITE:
For the May 1973 issue of *House & Garden,* Gloria decorated a bathroom that featured her collection of flower prints designed for Bloomcraft.

The New York Times Magazine

THE MARKETING OF GLORIA VANDERBILT

Not that the gifted writer from Quitman, Mississippi, who looked and acted as gallant as Prince Charming, was ever anything but his own man. He radiated a kindness and humor that affected everyone who knew him. He was so utterly supportive of all of Gloria's endeavors that their time together was one of the most productive and shining periods in her life. In his foreword to *Gloria Vanderbilt Book of Collage* (1970), Wyatt's tribute to his wife includes the following: "She moves on strange planes, that girl; she is a creature of some other mystery not altogether of this world, part wood nymph, part Earth Mother, and part American Beauty rose. She has the freshness of Snow White and the glamour of the Wicked Queen. She is as exotic as a unicorn and as subtle as an Egyptian temple cat. She is as crisp as gingham, as sensuous as satin, and as inscrutable as velvet. She is also as tentative as a doe in the forest, as delicate as a spider's web, as glittering as frost on a windowpane, and as pliant as a willow…. If she has not made of herself a living work of art, she's come damned close, or as close as anybody I'd ever want to meet."[2] Wyatt's book *Families: A Memoir and a Celebration* was published in 1975 with the following dedication: "To my two families, the one that made me and the one I made."[3] Gloria says, "Through Wyatt I came to know what family meant. What it means for a woman to raise children with their father by your side. What it means to face the world when you are not alone. He was the love of my life."[4]

OPPOSITE:
The December 1969 issue of *House & Garden* celebrated Gloria's extraordinary style at home, illustrating how she decorated her townhouse during the holiday season. Here, she is in the dining room with son Carter Cooper.

ABOVE:
Gloria designed the collage for the jacket of Wyatt Cooper's *Families: A Memoir and a Celebration*, published in 1975.

Truman Capote wrote of Wyatt's book, "An original and wise and very amusing account of the meaning to one man of his kin blood relationships in our world today. It's like sitting down before a fire and listening to the candid and warming conversation of a close friend who happens to be one of the most civilized men in the world."[5]

Wyatt was a devoted stepfather to Stan and Chris, who were soon joined by baby brothers. Carter Vanderbilt Cooper was born on January 27, 1965, followed by Anderson Hays Cooper on June 3, 1967. After Gloria had sold the south penthouse at 10 Gracie Square, she and Wyatt had bought a magnificent townhouse at 45 East Sixty-seventh Street, which would be the scene of some of the most lavishly beautiful entertaining in the city. Their Christmas parties were legendary, as was Gloria's wildly eclectic and brilliant decoration of this home. The patchwork master bedroom is still remembered as one of the great contemporary interiors. Gloria cut up who knows how many quilts to make curtains and completely cover the floor, walls, and ceiling with fabric. "We used very old patches on the walls, but we did not destroy fabric designs that were important," Gloria explained to Donald Miller in an interview.[6] To this day, no one has ever been able to replicate it. The lacquered patchwork fabric floor brings to mind Gloria's enchantment with Juliana Force's primrose path on Eighth Street.

ABOVE LEFT:
Ernst Beadle's cover for the December 1969 issue of *House & Garden* featured the East Sixty-seventh Street townhouse in all its festive glory.

ABOVE RIGHT:
Gloria and Wyatt Cooper were married in 1963 and created many extraordinary houses together. After their marriage, they bought a limestone townhouse at 45 East Sixty-seventh Street, where they hosted the most beautiful parties in the city. The Christmas card for 1967 featured a Cris Alexander photograph of the family at home: Stan is to the left of Wyatt, and Chris is standing to his right; Anderson is on Gloria's lap, playing with his brother Carter's hair.

OPPOSITE:
Gloria has always been famous for her sense of original style; here the table is set for a dinner party using a quilt as a tablecloth.

OPPOSITE & ABOVE:
Gloria and Wyatt's bedroom at 45 East
Sixty-seventh Street was one of the most
famous rooms in modern decoration. Here
Gloria covered every surface of the room
with a collage of quilt pieces, including the
lacquered floor. Horst P. Horst photographed
Gloria in an outfit designed by Adolfo
inspired by the room. The images appeared
in the February 1970 issue of *Vogue*.

ABOVE & OPPOSITE:

Two views of Gloria's master bedroom
completely covered in quilt fabric. The
patchwork floors were inspired by Juliana
Force's lacquered floors in her apartment
above the original Whitney Museum
of American Art on Eighth Street.

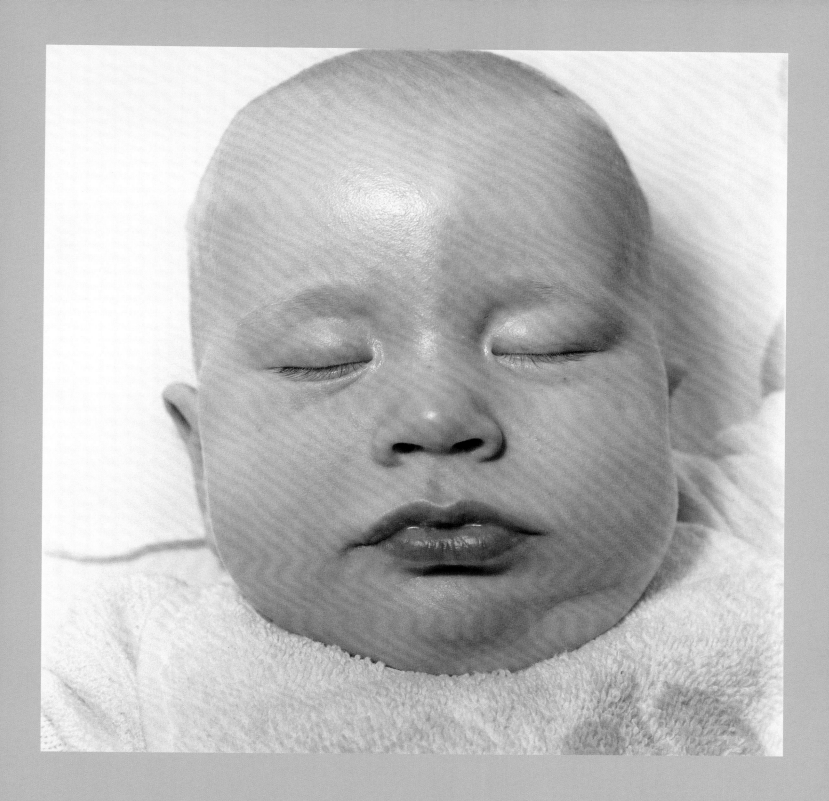

As beautiful as this house was, it was first and foremost a hearth, filled with friends and—most importantly—accommodating the family's activities. When he was a young aspiring rock musician, Stan remembers, "Mom let us rehearse at Sixty-seventh Street. In a way, I couldn't believe she was letting us do it. We set up in the dining room. And no comments about long hair and stuff like that, no problem…she was part of that whole thing. She was caught up in the spirit of the 1960s and understood it really well."[7] Gloria not only brought Stan and Chris to Carnegie Hall to hear the Beatles, but she also entered fully into the fantastical realm of psychedelic exploration when she took a doctor-monitored LSD trip in 1964.

When they sold the townhouse in 1974, Gloria and Wyatt moved the family to a modern apartment in the United Nations Plaza. Yet even in this glass-walled aerie, Gloria lived "in a print-lined floating bubble,"[8] as Brendan Gill wrote in *Vogue* in June 1975, using many of the fabrics she had designed. The Horst photographs that accompanied this story illustrated Gloria's aesthetic at its most exuberant.

Their happiness and partnership spilled over to the creation of two other fantastic houses for their family. The first was a fairy-tale stone house on sixteen acres in the woods by the Mianus River in Connecticut. They called the house Faraway. Toni Frissell photographed this house for *Vogue* in 1966. The photographs cast a spell, showing Gloria and her family in a dreamscape of natural and man-made beauty. Gloria's greeting to her baby son, "Hello, Super-Duper Carter Cooper," is just one of the many details in the Frissell story that convey a picture of family happiness.

OPPOSITE:
Gloria and Wyatt relaxing at their country house, Faraway, in Connecticut. The photograph was taken by Toni Frissell in 1965 for *Vogue*.

ABOVE:
Gloria stands midstream during
the Toni Frissell shoot for *Vogue*
at Faraway. The stone house was
hidden away in a fairy-tale setting.

Toni Frissell

OPPOSITE:
Gloria and Wyatt relax with the boys
in the living room at Faraway.

ABOVE:
The master bedroom was in the
stone tower of the house. The bed
is layered with Porthault linens.

ABOVE:
Brendan Gill wrote a story for *Vogue*
in 1975 about the U.N. Plaza apartment.
Horst took the photographs. Gill wrote
that "she lives in a print-lined 'floating
bubble,' her own works coexisting happily
with her possessions." Gloria covered
the kitchen walls with her own fabric.

OPPOSITE:
When Gloria and Wyatt moved the family
to the U.N. Plaza in 1974, she didn't let
the glass curtain walls inhibit her sense
of style. Here she decorated the living
room with her own fabric designs.

When Gloria and Wyatt felt that the boys needed to be closer to friends their own age, they sold Faraway and bought a house in Southampton, New York, said to have been designed in 1895 by Stanford White for his mother; they called this home Summertime. Gloria's genius for decorating with a totally free hand ruled here. She took gingham fabric and draped the master bedroom with it in much the same way she had applied the patchwork in New York. In a famous Francesco Scavullo portrait of Gloria at Summertime, she looks like the heroine of a John Singer Sargent painting. Gloria's great friend, *New York Times* chief theater critic Ben Brantley, observes, "She has created these marvelous shells for herself all along. She has created a moveable pageant. It is not that she is in retreat from the world, but she always has that sanctuary, and it is a great privilege to be invited into it, and it accommodates so many different kinds of people."[9]

There was an exciting convergence in Gloria's life during her marriage to Wyatt. She was at the peak of her powers as a designer of paper and home décor products, while creating her art and writing many books. Gloria and Wyatt were photographed everywhere they went. Gloria had been on the Best-Dressed List since 1966, and in 1969 fashion arbiter and list founder Eleanor Lambert dubbed Gloria and Wyatt the first Best-Dressed Couple. When the announcement was made, they were photographed strolling down the street in matching maxi coats, Wyatt's by Bill Blass and Gloria's by Adolfo. "The best-dressed men in town are the doormen," Eugenia Sheppard quoted Wyatt as saying in her *New York Post* column "Inside Fashion." "Their coats are really marvelously cut."[10]

Wyatt, like Gloria, sported his own fashion daring and élan. He was credited as "the first New Yorker to wear a Nehru jacket to a theater preview."[11] Wyatt was also listed on the first Best-Dressed List for men, joining Prince Philip, Bill Blass, Hubert de Givenchy, Cecil Beaton, and the Baron Alexis de Rede, among others. That same year Gloria was among the recipients of the thirty-first annual Neiman-Marcus Fashion Awards, along with Bill Blass, Emanuel Ungaro, Anne Klein, and Bernard Kayman.

Gloria's fashion evolution had started back in Hollywood when she wore clothes designed by Howard Greer, who had dressed her idol, Rita Hayworth. He designed what came to be known as "the tabletop dress," as stars had to look good from the waist up when they were photographed at restaurants.[12] She also wore

174.

OPPOSITE:
This portrait of Gloria on the balcony of Summertime, by Scavullo, calls up a modern John Singer Sargent painting. One of Gloria's collage works, *Gingham Queen Elizabeth*, hangs on the wall.

GLORIA VANDERBILT will come as a swan to Nashville's famous Swan Ball on Saturday night. **Adolfo** has made her dress of slinky white net with long, tight sleeves and a swirl of white feathers around the top. With it she'll wear what she likes to call the old family rhinestones and she'll carry a white feather fan.

Even without the feathers, Gloria's white skin and her long, slender neck suggest a swan. She is so slim nowadays that one of her friends says, "She is so narrow that she always seems to be standing in profile."

"No, I haven't been dieting," says Gloria who is 5-7½ and weighs 98 pounds. "It just happened. I was terribly busy getting ready for a museum show of my paintings and finishing my fabrics for Bloomcraft. In the mornings I just drank a cup of coffee. I was working all day in my studio, so I ate a bowl of Granola, one of those health food cereals, with some milk. At night I had steak, vegetables and a diet pudding."

Though Gloria has never been even faintly plump, she weighed 115 when she started losing weight this time. "I feel fine. I don't want to lose any more, but I'm planning to stay this way," she says.

Gloria and her husband, **Wyatt Cooper**, will leave Thursday for Nashville, but their purpose isn't just to be guests of honor at parties, picnics and balls. Though they turn up at most important events in New York, the Coopers aren't madly party oriented. Gloria has chosen to become a serious painter and Wyatt has written the book for the "Anything Goes" revival, enlarged to contain many extra **Cole Porter** songs that will reach Broadway this fall.

Naturally there will be plenty of parties during Nashville's annual top social event, like the cocktail buffet Friday night by **Mr.** and **Mrs. Harrold Flintoff, Mr.** and **Mrs.** ___ Saturday luncheon and the Swan Ball itself ___ Ambassador and **Mrs. Guilford Dudley,** ___ Jarman will also be involved ___ to Gloria, though, ___ the historic

Post Photo by Bill Cunningham

Gloria Vanderbilt in the swan dress Adolofo has designed for her to wear at Nashville's Swan Ball.

for Hallmark. "The crowds were incredible. They were so enthusiastic about my work," she says.

There will probably be the same kind of reception for ___self collage kits that are coming out soon ___ new fabrics that Bloomcraft is introduc- ___a technique of her collages, the ___ draperies rather than ___ vying to use

(MAGAZINE PAGE SEVEN)

39

The Coopers

AUTUMN IN NEW YORK . . . A gray day for the new season in the greatest town.

There was the celebrated socialite, Gloria to her fashionable vest and skirt. There was

Va

Inside Fashion

ALL ABOUT GLORIA

EUGENIA SHEPPARD

"Every artist dreams of a museum show," says **Gloria Vanderbilt,** who can stop dreaming now. The Reading Public Museum and Art Gallery will show her collected work, starting with a black tie preview Saturday evening, April 24.

About one-third of the exhibition will be new. The rest will include some of her acrylics, collages and oils borrowed back from early collectors like **Gordon Parks, Harrison Salisbury, MacCauley Conner, Mrs. Samuel Peabody** and **Peter Schaefer.**

The 76 canvases, to be hung in three of the museum's galleries, represent six years ___ of her life, according to Gloria. "When I saw them stacked in our hallway, I could ___rdly believe it. I was up almost all night, going from one to another and remem-___g when I had painted each one."

___ong the new paintings will be the ___trait she has just finished, as well ___trait of her son, **Stan.** The son of ___Stokowski, Stan will soon be 21. ___ portrait. I feel it is a kind of ___f youth today," Gloria Vander-

___ old favorites in the show ___ of a child in a garden that ___wns. A collage loaned that ___overed with letters ___ memoirs of ___n coll-

comes ___ of his ___ make the ___ even more

___ion the tartar ___, peaked crown ___ a wide band of ___ome a completely ___ion. Wyatt Coop-___ly black lamb, but **___ Beatty** wears it in ___d **Nureyev** in velv-

___ael Strange, made a point of dressing exactly alike. They ___ had identical cl-

Post Photo by McCarte

Gloria and Wyatt Cooper agree on long coats, thou the lengths and the designers are different.

and men will have to do s ___thing about it besides b ___tie." One of his own solut ___ is a jacket that used to ___marine officer's dress b ___ He took off the insignia.

Unfortunately, a man ___likes to have his clothes st ___the same note as his wi ___doesn't have many char ___yet. Any imagination in m ___fashions is just getting un ___way.

It's encouraging, thou ___hat the big annual fash ___how early in February ___Philadelphia, to benefit t ___museum, has switched fr ___women's to men's fashions ___e first time this year. T ___mmittee has asked Wy ___be commentator.

___Town

___dame Gres taffeta b ___wn with huge puffed sleeve ___ong the guests were Spa ___ Ambassador Merry d ___ Mrs. T. Sufern Tailer ___frey Beane's dress with th ___er sequin top and whi ___ collar and skirt, Mr ___h Thomas M

Gloria Cooper gets down to the knitty-gritty

"**S**weaters are better." That's the theme of city fashionables this spring, as they get down to the knitty-gritty with sweater-dresses that plummet to the ankle line. Take Gloria Vanderbilt Cooper, for example. Once recognized for her love of colorful fashion details like neck ruffles, quilting and patchwork, Gloria has switched fashion images. Now down to a thistle-light 96 pounds, the dark-haired artist-socialite wears pencil-slim crocheted and hand-knit dresses from her favorite designer, Adolpho, in a wide range of moods. Recent evenings, she has worn, from left: a China-inspired red knit with her own collage of plastic and fake ivory beads and ornaments; accompanied by her husband, Wyatt, a crocheted longie with demure pink satin sash; and a dramatic knit in black and white with masses of rhinestones.

—Bill Cunningham

OPPOSITE:
Gloria and Wyatt were photographed
everywhere they went. They were the
first couple named when Eleanor Lambert
created the Best-Dressed Couples list in 1969.

ABOVE:
Gloria and Wyatt in Nantucket, where she
was having a show of her lace collages—
and for which she also dressed in lace.

clothes by Lanz of Salzburg, always adding her own flourish with accessories. Paul Flato was one of her favorite jewelry designers. Gradually Gloria's bohemian flair gave way to a more serious take on fashion, as she became a client of the elegant American couturier Mainbocher in the mid-1960s. But when she befriended Cuban-born fashion designer Adolfo F. Sardina in 1967, she broke the fashion mold completely.

Life magazine proclaimed, "A vastly talented Vanderbilt shows off a new way of dressing." Scavullo photographed Gloria in Adolfo clothing inspired by her collage artwork. She wears a dashing mix of silver lamé harem pants and toe rings in one picture, while in another she dons a combination of thigh-high black leather pilgrim boots and Adolfo's "ribbon-festooned shirt and cape." The *Life* story goes on: "As a poet, actress, literary critic and artist, Mrs. Wyatt Cooper, better known as Gloria Vanderbilt, has often been called an up-to-date and very feminine version of the many-faceted Renaissance man."[13]

Today Adolfo says, "I think she is a woman who is always ahead of what is coming. She is always ahead of what is going to be." He remembers, "She was the first one to wear the long maxi coat, and then Mrs. Kennedy, who was still not married to Mr. Onassis—she called me and said, 'Oh, Adolfo, I saw Gloria Vanderbilt wearing one of your black coats. Please make me one exactly the same.'"[14] When Gloria and Wyatt hosted the launch party at their home, 45 East Sixty-seventh Street, to celebrate Gloria's position as Riegel Textile's new design director, they wore matching patchwork outfits by Adolfo.

ABOVE:
Life magazine featured a story on Gloria in 1968, writing that "a vastly talented Vanderbilt shows off a new way of dressing." She wears designs created for her by Adolfo, who found his inspiration in her creativity. Here, she is photographed with her artwork.

OPPOSITE:
Gloria on the cover of the February 1969 issue of *Town & Country*, photographed by Francesco Scavullo.

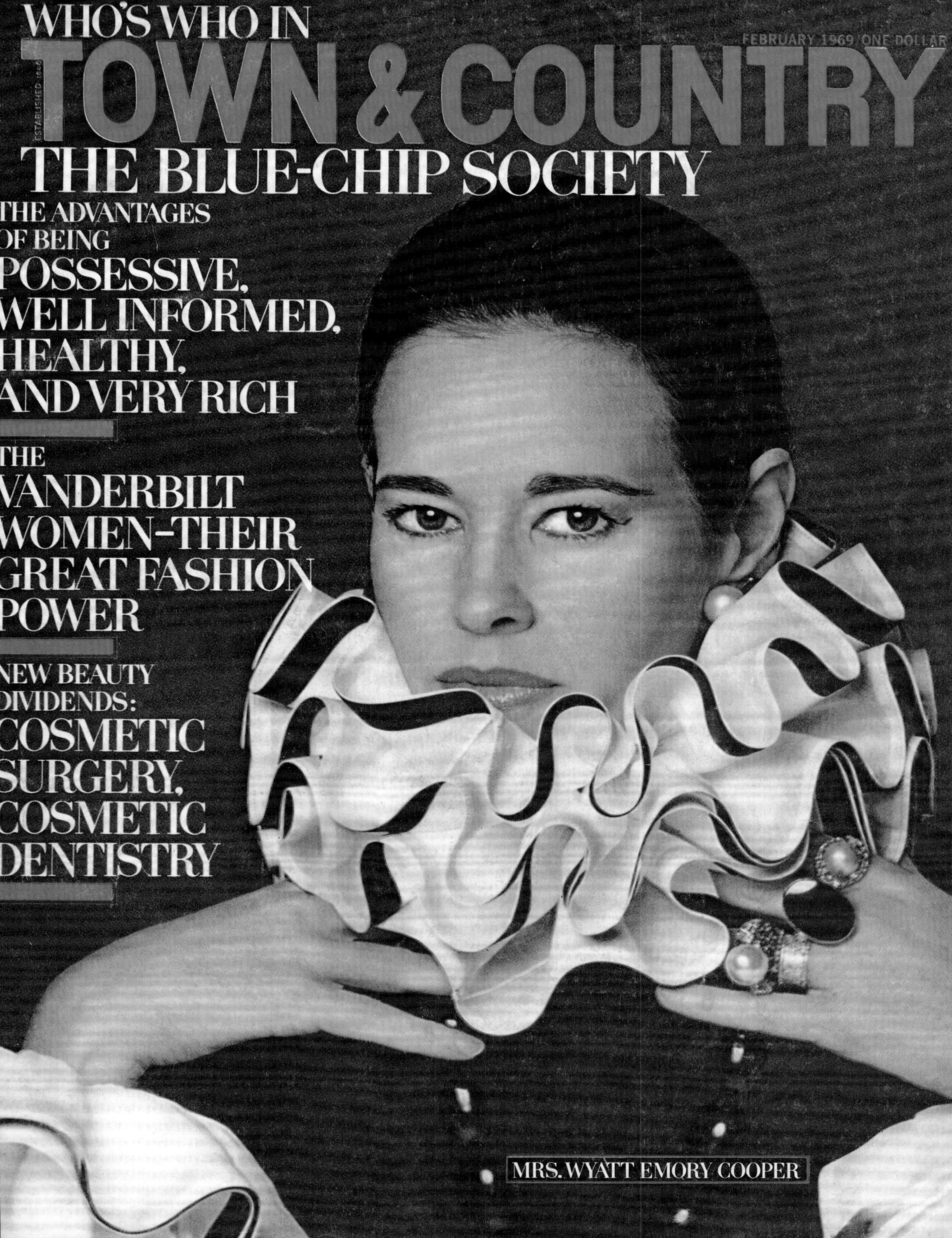
WHO'S WHO IN
FEBRUARY 1969/ONE DOLLAR
TOWN & COUNTRY
THE BLUE-CHIP SOCIETY
THE ADVANTAGES OF BEING POSSESSIVE, WELL INFORMED, HEALTHY, AND VERY RICH
THE VANDERBILT WOMEN–THEIR GREAT FASHION POWER
NEW BEAUTY DIVIDENDS: COSMETIC SURGERY, COSMETIC DENTISTRY
MRS. WYATT EMORY COOPER

Gloria was now a fashion icon. In 1969 Richard Avedon did a series of photographs for *Vogue* showing Gloria wearing her own Fortuny dresses. She accessorized each dress with her own jewelry designed by Rita Delisi. Harold Koda, head of the Costume Institute at the Metropolitan Museum of Art, says, "The images I think for me that were the most compelling were when she was wearing her Fortuny [dresses] and accessorizing them, because there the tendency would be to see Fortuny as classical, purely neoclassical, and what Gloria does so effectively is to go back to the Barbarian wearing ethnic jewelry in a way that doesn't talk about the bleached bones of antiquity, it's more about handwork." She has continued to champion great fashion designers, such as Zoran, who is known for his Spartan elegance. Koda adds, "Gloria Vanderbilt is an icon, because she not only had the happy circumstance of the very original look and the cultivated persona, but the partnership with some of the greatest photographers of the twentieth century."[15]

By the mid-1970s, Gloria's talent and her will to make her own way and her own living put her at the forefront of the fashion world. A shrewd Seventh Avenue businessman named Warren Hirsh called on Gloria after her dress line with Ben Shaw failed due to production problems. Hirsh was working for the Murjani brothers, whose Hong Kong factories produced jeans and shirts. When they recruited Hirsh in 1976 from Ship'n Shore, the Atlanta apparel company, their business was not a success. Hirsh cleaned up their inventory and started over with an idea. Hirsh recalls, "I said, 'What I would like to do is come up with a name that means something in the United States.' The name that came to me was Gloria Vanderbilt."[16] Her individual sense of style had already put her on the map, and Hirsh took note of the way Gloria put her own look together, especially

OPPOSITE:
Gloria Vanderbilt, dress by Fortuny, New York, June 1969
Photograph by Richard Avedon
Avedon photographed Gloria wearing her own Fortuny dresses for the December 1969 issue of *Vogue*. Each dress was accessorized with different jewelry designed by Rita Delisi. The description in *Vogue* reads: "sea-green silk, a jeweled tippet of carved green Jordanian stones and carved ivory beads suspended along gray silk floss from Mexican silver, ending in German silver hieratic figures."

the way she wore her Fiorucci jeans. Gloria in turn took Hirsh's idea of evolving the jeans market and created a new fit and styling, complete with her signature and swan logo. Together, Gloria and Hirsh launched the first-ever designer jeans at—where else?—Studio 54, the iconic 1970s disco where fashion and society became one. *New York* magazine rated the fit of Gloria Vanderbilt jeans number one in a poll published in 1979.

Gloria Vanderbilt Jeans took on a life of its own, because Gloria *was* Vanderbilt Jeans. She appeared in every single television commercial, including one with the pianist and cabaret singer Bobby Short. She tirelessly made store appearances around the country and abroad. The launch of Gloria Vanderbilt Jeans in Great Britain took place in the House of Lords, no less. Gloria led the pack, before Calvin Klein and Brooke Shields. Her friend, Jane Gunther, who was married to the late author John Gunther, marvels today, "Imagine her energy to do all those things. It is just astonishing—and to have been able to make a lot of money. She has a lot of Vanderbilt genes."[17]

Francesca Stanfill, then a cub reporter, described the phenomenal success of Gloria Vanderbilt Jeans in her cover story for the *New York Times Magazine*. Stanfill reported, "Murjani, which launched the jeans in December 1977, has sold 'a little over six million pairs' this past year, according to Hirsh, and expects to sell about ten million in 1980. Last year's sales amounted to $30 million; this year the company expects to do $125 million."[18] Stanfill remembers traveling with Gloria during her public appearances at the time. "In those days it was almost the level of—a slightly lesser level, but still almost at the level, at that time—of Princess Diana. Gloria was American royalty. And it isn't just that she had that really magical American name; she is naturally an aristocrat. She is naturally glamorous. She is also disciplined. She knows how to create that aura about herself, always beautifully dressed."[19]

Just as this venture was skyrocketing, Wyatt died tragically of a heart ailment in 1978, the same year Gloria purchased the North Penthouse at 10 Gracie Square, the year before the jeans business turned into a fashion phenomenon. An episode out of a grown-up Grimms' horror tale followed. The trauma of Wyatt's

184.

OPPOSITE:
Gloria had become such a fashion icon that in 1976 she was approached by the businessman Warren Hirsh, who was working with the Murjani brothers, to create her own line of Gloria Vanderbilt designer jeans. Gloria was tireless in promoting her brand, appearing in every commercial and store promotion. Gloria remembers being horrified during this shoot; once the models were assembled wearing her jeans, the photographer asked them all to turn around and face downward.

loss prompted Gloria to seek professional help. Her physician recommended the psychiatrist Dr. Christ L. Zois; in time he enlisted a lawyer friend of his, Thomas A. Andrews, to convince Gloria to give them power of attorney over her business and finances. She writes of this horrendous episode: "What I was signing, it turned out, gave 50 percent of the shares of Gloria Concepts Inc. to A to Z Associates. By these means, Andrews and Dr. Zois swindled me out of my name and home furnishings license, and much money, and because Andrews had not paid my taxes, the Internal Revenue Service came in and took my house, my apartment—everything."[20] Gloria won the court case, and both men lost their professional licenses and were ordered to pay a settlement of $1.6 million—not a penny of which was ever paid.

Gloria's son Stan said recently, "She probably never told you this, but when, years ago, the house in Southampton had to be sold, the IRS got a decree to see her safe-deposit boxes in Southampton because they probably thought they were full of diamonds. My mother asked me if I would meet them at the bank. I went and they brought out these boxes, and in these boxes there were cards and drawings that Chris and I had done over the years for her. That was all that was in there, packed in there. That shows what she valued."[21]

Bill Blass helped Gloria through this challenging period until she emerged with her fighting spirit, Carter and Anderson by her side, busy, and, as always, productive.

Then in the summer of 1988, Gloria's world went dark. On July 22, a ferociously hot day, Carter announced that he wanted to move back home to 10 Gracie Square. He had graduated from Princeton the year before and gotten a job as an editor at *American Heritage* magazine. He had been depressed by the recent breakup of a serious relationship. Although he rarely napped in the afternoon (he had sleepwalking episodes as a child), he fell asleep on the sofa in the library, asking that the air-conditioning not be turned on. Hours later, he came into Gloria's room, disoriented and dazed, in a trancelike state, repeatedly asking her, "What's going on? What's going on?" Suddenly he ran up the stairs to the terrace on the fourteenth floor, and Gloria, sensing something terrible was happening, ran after him. She describes what followed in her book *A Mother's Story*: "I stood there

187.

HOUSE & GARDEN

THE MAGAZINE OF CREATIVE LIVING FEBRUARY 1984 $4.0

ABOVE & RIGHT:

Gloria's living room in the north penthouse at 10 Gracie Square featured her portrait by Aaron Shikler and English chintz by Rose Cumming. The apartment was photographed by Edgar De Evia for the February 1984 issue of *House & Garden*.

OPPOSITE:

The living room also featured a George III mirror, a Louis XVI ormolu and marble clock, nineteenth-century German standing horn cups, and Victorian shells.

191.

LEFT:
Gloria's romantic bedroom featured
a draped canopy bed and a wall
covering by Rose Cumming.

afraid to move, afraid it would send him down—shouting 'Carter, Carter.' Then suddenly a helicopter passed above us, high up in the fading summer light—he looked directly up as if it were a signal, then turned and reached his hand out yearningly to me, and I moved towards him, my hand reaching for his, but as I did he moved, deftly as an athlete, over the wall, holding on to a cliff as if it were a practice bar in a gym. He firmly and confidently held on to the ledge, hanging down over the fourteen-story building—suspended there. 'Carter, come back,' I shouted, and for a moment I thought he was going to. But he didn't—he let go."[22]

192.

A Mother's Story details Gloria's journey from the darkest place any mother could ever know. Gloria says that after her custody trial, when Dodo was taken away from her, "I thought nothing that bad could ever happen to me again, and of course Carter died and it was more terrible."[23] But even when faced with the worst tragedy imaginable, Gloria willed herself back to life, back into a process of moving forward, seeking the will to go on. She transcended her personal grief and shared her experience in order to help others: "Don't give up, don't ever give up, because without pain there cannot be joy, and both are what make us know we are alive. You have the courage to let the pain you feel possess you, the courage not to deny it, and if you do this, the day will come when you wake and know that you are working through it, and because you are, there is a hope, small though it may be, a hope you can trust, and the more you allow yourself to trust it, the more it will tell you that although nothing will ever be the same, and the suffering you are working through will be with you always—you *will* come through, and when you do you'll know who you really are, and someday there will be moments when you will be able to love again, and laugh again, and live again. I hope this will come true for you as it has for me."[24]

Gloria's friend Diane von Furstenberg says, "Even though she has gone through such tragedy and such extremes, she has managed to remain pure, she has managed to remain enthusiastic and alive, and that is what I think is so beautiful about her. She has a child thing about her. She is so youthful. She still believes in romance. She is extraordinary."[25]

OPPOSITE:
Kenneth Paul Block's watercolor illustration of the living room in the north penthouse apartment at 10 Gracie Square, with Aaron Shikler's portrait of Gloria at the far end of the room. The illustration appeared in *W* in March 1983.

7.

RENEWAL

"God, what a fighter you are. I am so proud of you."

—RICHARD AVEDON, LETTER TO
GLORIA VANDERBILT ON JANUARY 12, 2004

I didn't expect her to be the traditional mom," Anderson Cooper says, sitting in his office at CNN in New York. "The scale she lives in is sort of different from other people, and I am not talking about financially; just her eyes are open wider, I think, than a lot of other people's, so she has this sense that anything is possible. She does believe that anything is possible. I always see that as a positive and a negative. I mean, anything is possible; horrible things can happen as well as great things. I think she only imagines great things."[1]

Imagining great things in the midst of what could have been catastrophic circumstances has been one of the many gifts in Gloria Vanderbilt's extraordinary life. Anderson remembers asking his mother for advice when he was trying to figure out his own life and career. "'Follow your bliss,'" he says with a smile.

OPPOSITE:
Gloria's painting
Geranium, 2006.

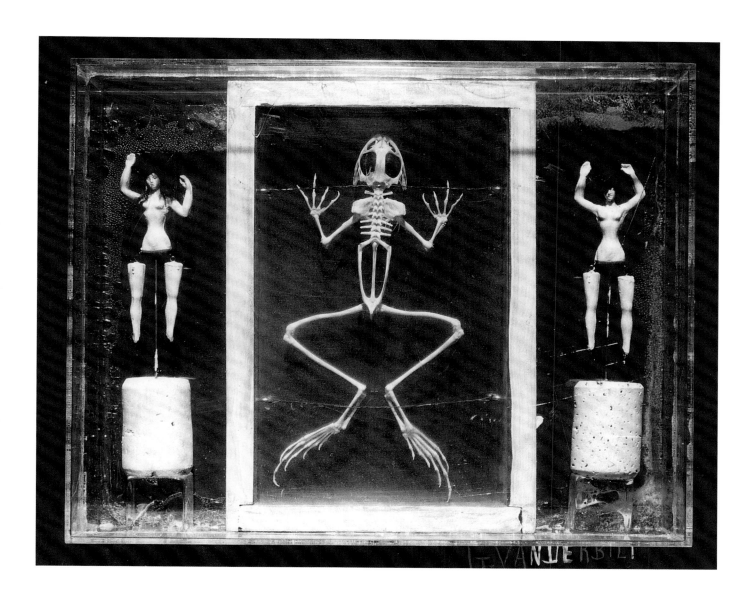

OPPOSITE & ABOVE:
Gloria's painting depicting herself and Dodo in the happy days when the Caravan was still intact hangs above the work desk in her present-day studio. A photographic portrait of her friend Joyce Carol Oates hangs to the left. Gloria's workspace comprises two rooms filled with completed works and objects that inspire or will be used in her inventive creations. The haven of her many studios has allowed Gloria to produce artwork of impressive scope and merit. Her collage *Memory* was made into a commemorative stamp by the United Nations to support the World Health Organization and UNICEF. She has received honorary Doctorates of Fine Arts and awards including the National Society of Arts & Letters Gold Medal of Merit and the Anti-Defamation League Woman of Achievement award. Her work has been shown in museums and galleries across the country. Gloria continues to create—painting, making collage, and building Dream Boxes (a recent piece, *Untitled* [1998], is pictured above)—as outlets for her vision and imagination.

"You want something more specific—like 'plastics,' but of course that is the best advice there is. I am pleased she was watching Joseph Campbell, and not Montel Williams," he deadpans, "because God knows what advice I would have gotten. She was watching the Bill Moyers interview with Campbell and that is where 'follow your bliss' comes from."[2]

Gloria's bliss has been hard won and there was no one there to give her advice, ever, and yet she instinctively knew that you have to find bliss on your own.

When she was recently asked if she could recall her first memory, Gloria answered: "Well, my first memory is of my mother, and it's the only time that I ever remember that we did something together, painting a cigar box made of wood, and decorating it with various bits and pieces of flowers she cut out of magazines and that kind of thing, and we were painting the box a bright yellow and the room was flooded with sunlight—oh God, she was beautiful, and I remember being really happy."[3]

OPPOSITE:

The portrait of Gloria's mother, painted by
Dana Pond in Paris in 1923, is in the living
room of her apartment and has traveled with
her over the years wherever she has lived.

Today she reflects: "As a child, although
I saw little of her, I fell in love with my
mother's beauty, longing to be close to
her, but there was nobody home. And later
when Naney Morgan manipulated me to
fear her, I obsessed about her, conflicted by
feelings of anger and hostility, yet wanting
her love and approval. Estranged from
her until mid-life, when I found courage to
reconcile with her, she stood before me as
a stranger, tentative, passive. I accepted
without complaint the 'hysterical blindness'
that had claimed her long ago, a 'conversion'
disorder, which is real to the afflicted
person and cannot be explained by any
neurological or medical reason. The physical
symptoms, which include blindness, are
believed to be the result of psychological
conflicts translated into physical symptoms.
We never came to know each other before
she died three years later, but not a day
passes that I do not think about her, and
as I do, my relationship with her keeps
changing. I try to understand and suspect
that it wasn't my fault—perhaps she was
capable only of loving her twin sister
Thelma, the mirror image of herself."

One wishes that there had been a bouquet of happy memories from which to choose. But the one thing that is evident in Gloria Vanderbilt's life is that her strength and resolve and invincible warrior spirit didn't come from the wasteland of imagining "what if." Her incredible journey has been built on dealing with "what is," and the hard work and courage it takes to transform the uncontrollable in life into something positive and enriching. André Breton's observation that "childhood is the only reality" is the mountain that has to be scaled in life. Some make it over and others do not. The vulnerabilities of Gloria's mother—who Wyatt Cooper observed "never understood one thing that ever happened to her,"[4]—have never been washed away. "I fell in love with her beauty and forever after sought it, longed for it and often found it in people and in the beauty of objects and rooms, and bonded with these things as a way of being close to her," Gloria says today. She concludes that "I spent the rest of my life obsessing about her, but in midlife, estranged for seventeen years, found the courage to reconcile with her. The shock of the mother I had been manipulated to fear stood before me,

ABOVE:
An original Mainbocher label adorns Gloria's vanity mirror.

OPPOSITE:
Gloria's living room mantel is one of her many ongoing painting projects at home. Her painting above the fireplace had been bought years ago by Richard Avedon; after his death, it was included in an auction and Anderson bought the painting back for his mother, along with a sculpture by Avedon's mother, *Ovum*.

LEFT:
Gloria's *Heart's Desire* (2008) is an oversized Dream Box sculpture. The cube construction (measuring seventy-two feet on all sides) is on permanent view at the Grounds for Sculpture, founded by J. Seward Johnson, in Hamilton, New Jersey.

PAGE 204:
Gloria painted the tiles in one of her studio bathrooms in the 1990s.

PAGE 205:
A glimpse of Gloria's collection of dolls and doll heads, which she incorporates into her artwork

tentative—vulnerable. Never speaking of events that happened between us, never becoming close, she died three years later. Not a day passes that I do not think of her, and as I do, my relationship with her keeps changing, as I try to understand the forces that came between us, and this assuages the longing for that which I never had."[5]

Gloria's feelings about the loss of her father are starker. "I didn't miss a father, having no knowledge that such a person existed." It was only when Gloria went to visit her cousin Bill Vanderbilt (then governor of Rhode Island) and his wife (known to their children as Mummy Anne) at Oakland Farm in Newport that "the concept of having a father dawned on me. Until then, having never seen fathers with my friends in Paris—Betsy Drake, Peter Salm—it never occurred to me that there were families who had a mother and a father. Here I came upon it close at hand, and it was a revelation ... a happy family consisting of a mother and father. This is when I started being intensely curious about something I never had."[6]

The world of Gloria Vanderbilt has been built from a rich collage of memory and experience, producing a unique universe she extends to her family and friends, and then to the larger world beyond through her art. Her friend Marti Stevens puts it this way: "She has the willpower, and of course, she is her own very best creation. Art springs from her fingertips. When you go into that magical apartment, you walk into an entirely different world of absolute beauty. She lives within the boundless terrain of her amazing imagination. I can't wait until she says, 'Oh, come over, there is something I want to show you.'"[7]

Today Gloria's life is busier than ever. She is writing and painting in preparation for more books and exhibitions. Her apartment is a constantly evolving personal landscape, filled with her passion for family, photographs, artwork, color, textiles, books, and flowers. It remains truly a moveable feast, as she takes her paintbrush at whim to decorate mantels and window frames, incorporating new treasures into the décor.

OPPOSITE:
A corner of Gloria's bedroom, with her *Silver Elizabeth* collage work above the Max Kuene painted chest. A string of her mother's amethyst beads lies on the books.

PAGES 208–209:
Annie Leibovitz photographed Gloria and Anderson for a story in the June 2006 issue of *Vanity Fair*.

And just when you might have thought Gloria Vanderbilt had played the most astonishing hand of her creative life, she springs forward with yet another surprise. In 2009 her erotic novel *Obsession* was published, earning a glowing article in the *New York Times* by Charles McGrath.[8] And she is always in love. "I have never met anyone past the age of sixteen who so loves being in love," Ben Brantley says. "It is an intransitive state with her. If you are looking for a key to eternal youth, that is it!"[9] Her friend Ellen "Pucky" Violett, who has known her since their days at the Greenvale School, states, "Nothing Gloria Vanderbilt ever does in this lifetime is ever going to surprise me. She is just too amazing, and you cannot put her in a category. You cannot confine her to a corner."[10]

Gloria's family is her great pride. Stan lives with his wife, Emily, and their son, Myles, in eastern Long Island, where he has his own landscape garden design business called New Ground Gardens. His two daughters by his first marriage, Aurora and Abra Stokowski, live in Brooklyn. Stan is also a musician who has played with the band the xframes and is now playing with After the Carnival, as well as being part of a jazz jam in Sag Harbor every week. Chris has chosen to live apart from the family for the last few years. Anderson, the anchor for CNN's *Anderson Cooper 360°* and the author of the bestselling memoir *Dispatches from the Edge*, is one of the most respected and renowned television journalists in the world.

Gloria recently wrote to interior designer Matthew Patrick Smyth, a collaborator on various projects, describing a fantasy inspired by reading about her friend actor Joel Grey's house: "I must have a tiny secret house like that and it must be in Venice Beach. I will let my hair grow long and white and you will help me decorate it and there will be a tiny guest cottage painted sea blue-green with stars and a moon and a yellow sun on the ceiling and I will paint during the day and at night dance with friends on the beach and in the garden will be a gazebo, very lacey curlicues painted silver with vines of night-scented jasmine twining over as we sit having jasmine tea on a misty afternoon . . . oh, I must stop before I get completely carried away . . ."[11]

But that would not be before she has published another book, created art for another show, and invited you over, if you are lucky enough to enter her enchanted kingdom, greeting you at the door with a mysterious smile, looking like a modern angel with a treasured secret you may or may not ever get to know.

211.

OPPOSITE:
Gloria's writing desk is in her book-lined library, which doubles as a cozy dining area, where she entertains by candlelight.

ENDNOTES

1. GROWING UP VANDERBILT

1. *Life*, November 17, 1941, 143.
2. *Without Prejudice*, 31.
3. Ibid., 91.
4. E-mail to the author, January 29, 2010.
5. *Without Prejudice*, 91.
6. Ibid., 115.
7. Ibid., 116.
8. *The Vanderbilts*, 270.
9. *Gertrude Vanderbilt Whitney*, 11.
10. *The Vanderbilts*, 27.
11. Ibid., 30.
12. *Gertrude Vanderbilt Whitney*, 13.
13. Ibid., 14.
14. *Great Houses of New York*, 26.
15. Ibid., 38.
16. *New York Times*, November 26, 1893.
17. *Gilded Mansions*, 163.
18. E-mail to the author, January 20, 2010.
19. *Without Prejudice*, 37.
20. Interview with the author, September 25, 2009.
21. *Once Upon a Time*, 1.
22. *Without Prejudice*, 132.

2. LEARNING THE SONGS OF THE CARAVAN

1. Interview with the author, February 1, 2009.
2. Ibid.
3. Ibid.
4. Ibid.
5. Ibid.
6. Ibid.
7. *Once Upon a Time*, 4.
8. *Without Prejudice*, 129.
9. Ibid., 137.
10. Ibid., 138.
11. *King Edward VIII*, 12.
12. *Once Upon a Time*, 21.
13. Ibid.
14. Ibid., 29.
15. E-mail to the author, January 29, 2010.
16. *Once Upon a Time*, 49.
17. Ibid., 51.
18. Interview with the author, January 29, 2010.
19. Ibid.
20. Ibid.

3. COMING HOME

1. E-mail to the author, January 20, 2010.
2. Ibid.
3. *Once Upon a Time*, 224.
4. E-mail to the author, January 20, 2010.
5. *Once Upon a Time*, 261.
6. Ibid., 211.
7. Ibid., 247.
8. *It Seemed Important at the Time*, 14.
9. *Black Knight, White Knight*, 26.
10. *It Seemed Important at the Time*, 15.
11. Interview with the author, February 13, 2009.
12. *It Seemed Important at the Time*, 20.
13. *Black Knight, White Knight*, 84.
14. E-mail to the author, January 29, 2010.
15. Ibid.
16. Interview with the author, February 13, 2009.

4. BUILDING NEW KINGDOMS

1. Interview with the author, February 20, 2009.
2. *Black Knight, White Knight*, 107.
3. Ibid., 141.
4. Ibid., 146.
5. E-mail to the author, August 31, 2009.
6. *Black Knight, White Knight*, 219.
7. Interview with the author, June 12, 2009.
8. *Black Knight, White Knight*, 220.
9. Ibid., 236.
10. Interview with the author, February 20, 2009.
11. *Black Knight, White Knight*, 250.
12. *It Seemed Important at the Time*, 60.

5. SHOWTIME

1. *Black Knight, White Knight*, 276.
2. Jess Stearn, "Gloria Vanderbilt Steps Out," *Daily News*, December 28, 1954.
3. *New York Journal-American*, January 20, 1955.
4. *Black Knight, White Knight*, 297.
5. *It Seemed Important at the Time*, 81.
6. Interview with the author, February 13, 2009.
7. E-mail to the author, August 10, 2009.
8. E-mail to the author, August 24, 2009.
9. *Woman to Woman*, 80.
10. Interview with the author, June 28, 2009.
11. *It Seemed Important at the Time*, 92.
12. Interview with the author, February 13, 2009.
13. E-mail to the author, August 23, 2009.

6. VANDERBILT GENES

1. Interview with the author, August 31, 2009.
2. *Gloria Vanderbilt Book of Collage*, 9.
3. *Families*, dedication.
4. Interview with the author, January 29, 2010.
5. *Families*, jacket.
6. "Collage Kits Shown by Gloria Vanderbilt," *Pittsburgh Post-Gazette*, September 13, 1972.
7. Interview with the author, June 28, 2009.
8. "Gloria Vanderbilt Updated," *Vogue*, June 1975.
9. Interview with the author, May 25, 2009.
10. "The Long Coats Are Coming," *New York Post*, 1969.
11. Marilyn Bender, "24 on New List of World's 10 Best-Dressed," *International Herald Tribune*, January 15, 1969.
12. *Woman to Woman*, 71.
13. "Gloria's 'Bits and Pieces' Add Up to a Lot of Style," *Life*, October 4, 1968.
14. Interview with the author, July 7, 2009.
15. Interview with the author, August 10, 2009.
16. Interview with the author, June 8, 2009.
17. Ibid.
18. "The Marketing of Gloria Vanderbilt," *New York Times Magazine*, October 14, 1969.
19. Interview with the author, July 29, 2009.
20. *It Seemed Important at the Time*, 125.
21. Interview with the author, June 28, 2009.
22. *A Mother's Story*, 104.
23. Interview with the author, February 1, 2009.
24. *A Mother's Story*, 140.
25. Interview with the author, July 25, 2009.

7. RENEWAL

1. Interview with the author, September 25, 2009
2. Ibid.
3. Interview with the author, February 13, 2009.
4. Ibid
5. Interview with the author, February 25, 2009.
6. Ibid.
7. Interview with the author, January 16, 2010.
8. *New York Times*, June 18, 2009.
9. Interview with the author, July 15, 2010.
10. Ibid.
11. E-mail to Matthew Patrick Smyth, May 2, 2009.

OPPOSITE:

Gloria's collage painting *For Wyatt: Christmas 1969* hangs in her apartment. To the right is a sculpture of fashion designer Valentina by Sally Ryan.

214.

ACKNOWLEDGMENTS

This book is dedicated to Nora Mulkerins Marley, with so much love and gratitude.

There are no words to thank Gloria Vanderbilt for the privilege, joy, and inspiration of working together to realize this book. I am indebted to Gloria's family, especially Stan Stokowski, Emily Goldstein, and Anderson Cooper, for their time, generosity, and support. I could not have found my way if it had not been for the amazing Nora and her daughter, GG. I am so grateful for the invaluable help and time I spent with Gloria's extended family of friends, including Anne Slater and John Cahill, Nancy Biddle, Jane Gunther, Marti Stevens, Diane von Furstenberg, Adolfo F. Sardiña, Harold Koda, Joyce Carol Oates, Ben Brantley, Francesca Stanfill, Helen "Pucky" Violett, Helen O'Hagan, Diane Volz, and Pearl Bedell. Thank you to Warren Hirsh, who masterminded Gloria Vanderbilt Jeans.

I cannot thank my dearest friend John Avedon enough for his support and generosity, and also Laura Avedon for her support and friendship. A special thanks to Matthew Patrick Smyth and Robert Rufino for being white knights, and to treasured Gray Foy, Joel Kaye, Lloyd Williams, and Richard Lee, who kept me going through the hardest part. My deepest thanks to Debra Kanabis and the team at Ralph Lauren, with a special thanks to Ralph Lauren for his generous support.

My thanks to the amazing Chip Kidd, whose exquisite design sensibility created this book. There are no words to thank Philip Reeser, "Prince Philip" to me, who has been such a support and friend and whose brilliance unearthed the photographs for the book, and Anne Longley, whose research, support, and friendship made all the difference. I am so grateful to my agent, Amanda Urban, and my heroes at Abrams: Michael Jacobs, Eric Himmel, Aiah Wieder, Michelle Ishay, Shawn Dahl, Katrina Weidknecht, and Sylvia P. Barnes, who makes me happy every time I walk in the door. My deepest gratitude to the remarkable photographer, Ditte Isager, who photographed Gloria's world today. A special thanks to Annie Leibovitz, Doon Arbus, and Lillian Bassman, and to Jerome K. Walsh for his wisdom and guidance. A very special thanks to the incredible generosity and help from Robert B. King and Charles Marlor, whose insights and research have been such a gift, and to Norma Stevens for her wonderful help in getting it all started. I am so grateful to Andrew Wiley, Paul Roth, James Martin, Michelle Franco, Christopher Nesbit, Miyuki Tsushima, Clemency Cook, Shelley Dowell, and everyone at the Richard Avedon Foundation for their invaluable help and the great privilege of featuring the Richard Avedon photographs.

This book has been made possible by the help and generosity of Leigh Montville, Shawn Waldron, Cynthia Cathcart, Florence Palomo, Marianne Brown, Dawn Lucas-Carlson, Molly Monosky, and Jane Larkworthy at Condé Nast. Thank you so much to Michael Shulman at Magnum Photos, Susan Kriete at the New-York Historical Society, Barbara Briggs-Anderson at Loon Hill Studios, David McJonathan at the Edgar de Evia Archive, Stella Benakis at Francesco Scavullo Editions, Daniel Cheek at Fraenkel Gallery, John Pelosi at the Diane Arbus Estate, Jesse Blatt at Annie Leibovitz Studio, Lizzie Himmel and Stephen Lipuma at Bassman Himmel Studio, Howard Mandelbaum and Brent Earle at Photofest, Dan Oppenheimer at Jack Robinson Archive, Elescia Wojak at Corbis, and Eric Rachlis at Getty Images.

I am so grateful to Richard David Story and all the fantastic editors who make it possible for me to do the work I love.

I especially want to thank, always, my editor-in-chief at *New York* magazine, the incredible Adam Moss, who inspires me to go further every single day. I am indebted to his generosity, which made it possible for me to take the time to write this book. Also I want to thank the wonderful Ann Clarke at *New York*, whose kindness and understanding is a constant beacon.

And as ever, my family, who are everything.

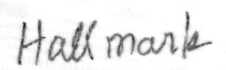

PHOTOGRAPH CREDITS

André Kertész / *House & Garden* / Condé Nast Archive; Copyright © Condé Nast: 78

© Annie Leibovitz, 2010: 208–9

Associated Press: 44

Associated Press / Photograph by John Lent: 122–23

© Bettmann/CORBIS: 39, 45 left and right, 70, 77 left, 97, 100, 126, 127, 130

Bob Adelman: 152 top and bottom

© Condé Nast Archive/CORBIS: 5, 119

© CORBIS: 28

© 1967 The Estate of Diane Arbus LLC: 165

Ditte Isager: 6, 7, 8, 13, 16, 26, 33, 58–59, 106, 147, 149, 150, 196, 198, 200, 201, 204, 205, 207, 210, 213, 218, 223, 224

Edgar de Evia / *House & Garden* / Condé Nast Archive; Copyright © Condé Nast: 154, 156 left, 157, 188 top & bottom, 189, 190–91

Photographs by Francesco Scavullo, Francesco Scavullo Foundation. www.scavulloeditions.com: 144, 175, 180, 181, 217

George Hurrell / *Vogue* / Condé Nast Archive; Copyright © Condé Nast: 82

© Courtesy of the Horst P. Horst Estate / Art + Commerce: 68

Horst P. Horst / *House & Garden* / Condé Nast Archive; Copyright © Condé Nast: 153

Horst P. Horst / *Vogue* / Condé Nast Archive; Copyright © Condé Nast: 151 top, 158, 159, 160, 161, 172, 173, 176

Inge Morath © The Inge Morath Foundation/Magnum Photos: 140, 141

Jack Robinson Archive: 10, 177

John Rawlings / *Vogue* / Condé Nast Archive; Copyright © Condé Nast: 111

Julian P. Graham/Loon Hill Studios: 90, 91

Courtesy Lillian Bassman: 114, 115

Collection of The New-York Historical Society, 83139d: 124

Courtesy Pointed Leaf Press, from *Drawing Fashion: The Art of Kenneth Paul Block*, 2008: 193

© 2010 Ricardo Barros: 202–3

© 2010 The Richard Avedon Foundation: jacket front, 14, 113, 120, 132, 133, 135, 136, 137, 138–39, 143, 182

Collection of Robert B. King & Charles S.L Marlor: 24, 27 top and bottom, 27, 30, 31, 32, 56–57, 72–73

Image courtesy of the Robert D. Farber University Archives & Special Collections Department, Brandeis University: 20–21

Photofest: 19, 86–87, 125

Popperfoto/Getty Images: 74

Time & Life Pictures/Getty Images: 61, 79, 83, 128, 185

Photograph by Timothy H. O'Sullivan, courtesy the Library of Congress: 37

Photograph by Toni Frissell: 164, 167, 168–69, 170, 171

All other photographs and objects appearing in this book have been provided by Gloria Vanderbilt from her own archive.

OPPOSITE:
A contact sheet from a sitting that Gloria did with Francesco Scavullo in the 1970s

INDEX

OPPOSITE:
Gloria's own hall of mirrors in her apartment, giving a glimpse of other rooms at every turn.

221.

Editors: Eric Himmel and Aiah Rachel Wieder
Design: Chip Kidd with Shawn Dahl, dahlimama inc
Production Manager: Anet Sirna-Bruder

Cataloging-in-Publication Data has been applied for
and may be obtained from the Library of Congress.
ISBN: 978-0-8109-9592-5

Printed and bound in Hong Kong, China
10 9 8 7 6 5 4 3 2 1

Abrams books are available at special discounts when
purchased in quantity for premiums and promotions
as well as fundraising or educational use. Special
editions can also be created to specification. For
details, contact specialmarkets@abramsbooks.com
or the address below.

THE ART OF BOOKS SINCE 1949
115 West 18th Street
New York, NY 10011
www.abramsbooks.com

OPPOSITE:
Gloria's initials, in her own brushstroke,
from one of her recent canvases

PAGE 224:
Gloria's 1957 self-portrait hangs in
the entrance of her studio today.

Editors: Eric Himmel and Aiah Rachel Wieder
Design: Chip Kidd with Shawn Dahl, dahlimama inc
Production Manager: Anet Sirna-Bruder

Cataloging-in-Publication Data has been applied for
and may be obtained from the Library of Congress.
ISBN: 978-0-8109-9592-5

Printed and bound in Hong Kong, China
10 9 8 7 6 5 4 3 2 1

Abrams books are available at special discounts when
purchased in quantity for premiums and promotions
as well as fundraising or educational use. Special
editions can also be created to specification. For
details, contact specialmarkets@abramsbooks.com
or the address below.

ABRAMS
THE ART OF BOOKS SINCE 1949
115 West 18th Street
New York, NY 10011
www.abramsbooks.com

OPPOSITE:
Gloria's initials, in her own brushstroke,
from one of her recent canvases

PAGE 224:
Gloria's 1957 self-portrait hangs in
the entrance of her studio today.

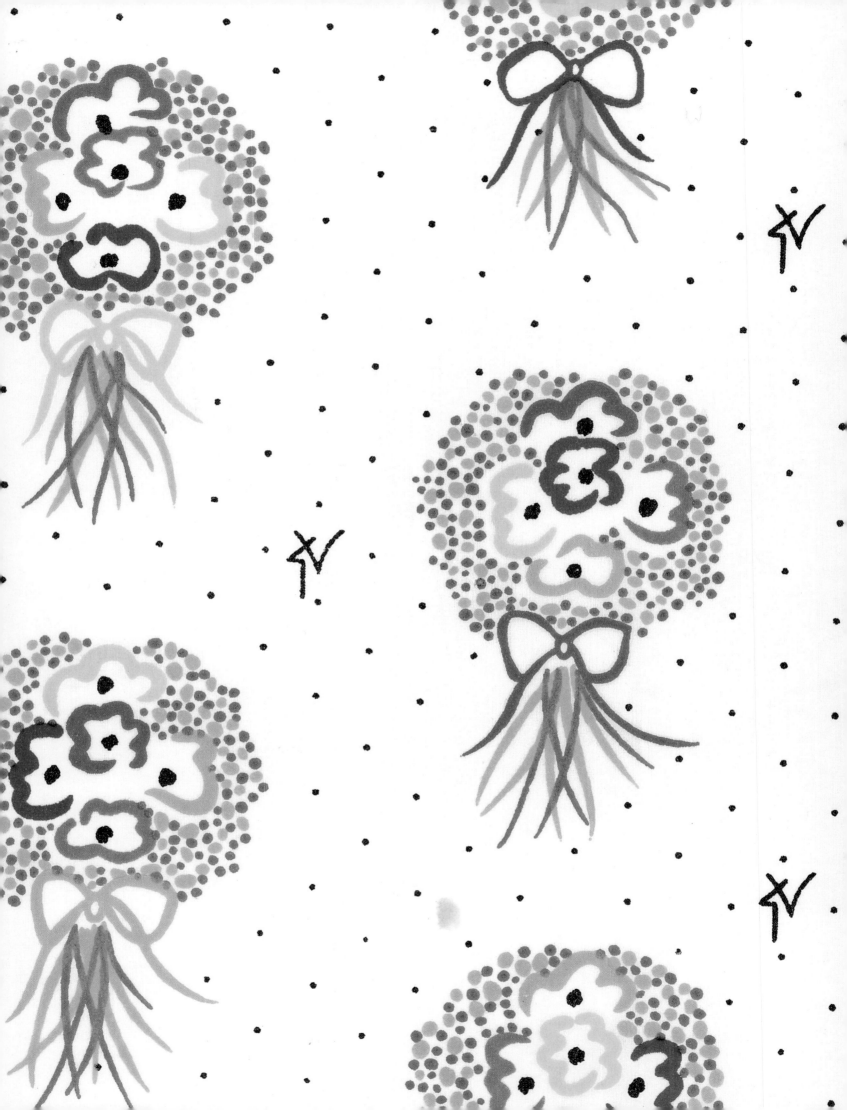